i am Desposynos I AM

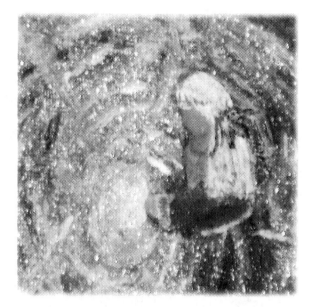

Book 1
Walking the RAINBOW Circle

by Sarah Mary Star

BALBOA.PRESS
A DIVISION OF HAY HOUSE

Balboa Press books may be ordered through booksellers or by contacting:

Balboa Press
A Division of Hay House
1663 Liberty Drive
Bloomington, IN 47403
www.balboapress.com
844-682-1282

Scripture quotations marked KJV are from the Holy Bible, King James Version (Authorized Version). First published in 1611. Quoted from the KJV Classic Reference Bible, Copyright © 1983 by The Zondervan Corporation.

ISBN: 979-8-7652-2663-6 (sc)
ISBN: 979-8-7652-2662-9 (e)

Library of Congress Control Number: 2022907741

Print information available on the last page.

Balboa Press rev. date: 03/29/2022

Contents

Dedication:

This book is dedicated to the Whole. It is for the ancient ones, who knew how to be in synchronicity with All That Is... those who knew the stillness between the breaths, and the peace between the heart-beats. For those who understood that there are no "separate individuals," only One Great All-Encompassing Being. It is for we who are now here, trying to find our own ways of experiencing our life paths. It is for my children and grandchildren, and for yours. They will inherit whatever legacy we may choose to leave for them. It is for the Earth Mother Herself.

I dedicate this book to assisting in restoring the balance, so imperative to our surviving and thriving. May we reclaim the dignity, strength, gentleness, and wholeness that we are. We are one... men, women and children of very race, culture, and creed. Nothing has ever been lacking in any of us. We have the capacity to not only survive, but to thrive. There are enough resources for every being of every species upon the face of Mother Earth to be healthy, happy, housed, fed and cared for. Sharing them is the key to rebalancing, healing, and triumphing over adversity, perhaps to our very survival.

Let us now know that miracles abound everywhere,
every moment! We are miraculous beings!

We now reclaim our Divinity! Expect miracles and they shall appear!

Mote it be so.

Foreword: Writing in Time…

This book began as a family anthology, a record of "us" for my kids and grandkids. Along the way, it decided to write itself into something else. Those of you who write, will understand this. Whether you are a novelist, a famous self-help guru, a romance writer, a poet… or you may be a journal keeper, with pages and pen by your bedside. You may even have years' worth of written anecdotes languishing in shoeboxes beneath your bed. This was my "reality" until a few years ago, when I began writing, rewriting and organizing the poetry and prose in those shoeboxes, researching my roots and honoring my dreams, visions and life experiences.

In any case, you will know, that as your hand holds the pen, or types away, words solidify on pages. Concepts and ideas that had existed until that moment only ethereally, enter the "real world" as words on paper. Mostly, they meander seemingly at will. They become adventures, poetry, romance, stories of the past, present or future. They excite us! They are energetic imprints, distilled by human hands. Sometimes, they seem familiar. Sometimes, not quite so… As if they created themselves…

I wrote, edited, and rewrote this manuscript dozens of times. I added, subtracted, omitted and rewrote large portions of it. It had to be *perfect* to be acceptable. It had to be formal, accurate, well researched and documented. Most writers can also identify with this aspect of writing.

Then, finally I figured it out. *I AM* (spirit self) all the time, even when *i am* (ego/ human self) is at the fore, leading my life in its less lofty ways. Much of the process was/ is my own journey of being. Of remembering who I am, and why I am choosing to be here at this time of transcending, or as author/ life coach Jim Kwik calls it, "trance ending."

I needed a good kick in the pants to get this book finished! *It just never seemed ready. I just never seemed ready.* I was still dragging my feet. And then… the times of change, *"The Great Awakening"* long foretold by the seers of humanity arrived, disguised as the Corona Virus (Covid-19). Much of this writing was done before Covid-19 appeared. It is still as valid as it was then. I have resisted the urge to expunge it as the *"Old Reality"* people talk about nervously, from socially distanced platforms. Rather, it stands on its own merit. We the people will, over the next months and years, decide what the highly anticipated *"New Reality"* will encompass.

The whole world is struggling to make sense of things. Great change is needed to restore some semblance of balance, of peace, of equality, of health. With the current political, religious, economic, social and climate chaos, no time to wait for just the right conditions to arise. Nothing new can emerge, until humanity is ready and able to let go of our current inequities and replace them with a balanced, compassionate, united World Circle. This is the task of every citizen of Mother Earth. We each and all are responsible for our part.

"Abracadabra"

We all know this word. It has been used by magicians the world over for a very long time, as they wave their magic wands! But where did it come from? What is its origin?

You might be surprised! It is derived from the words "avra kehdabra" in Aramaic, the language spoken by Yeshua/ Jesus and his family.

It translates as, "I will create as I speak."

Long ago, the people of Mother Earth understood the Oneness of All That Is. They saw no separation between themselves, the natural world, and the divine. Those notions crept into commonly accepted dogma, as societies became less spiritual (heart-based) and more scientific (mind-based). "Alaha" is the Aramaic word that Yeshua ben Youssef (Jesus Christ) used to describe the Oneness (God/Goddess). He repeatedly stated that everyone has the right and the ability to become as he was, a "Christ," an "Awakened One." As One with All That Is, how could it be otherwise!?! The "Kingdom of Heaven" was perceived as an inner state of being, not a faraway "place" to aspire towards if/ when worthy of it.

Human Beings have always wanted to belong to something bigger and more important than we may find in our day-to-day lives. We strive for a sense of fitting into a true and correct pack or tribe, under the umbrella of *"Spiritual Perfection."* In modern times, most of us have forgotten the Wisdom Teachings of the Ancient Ones. These valuable insights into Right Living are still alive within the elders, shaman, and seers of tribal cultures everywhere around the globe. Many centuries-old traditional practices and ceremonies survive. They hold keys to restoring balance, and to healing the great cosmic wounds we humans have created.

Modern spiritual teachers, as they remember and re-turn (turn again) to themselves, are assisting the masses to awaken. Many are travelling around Mother Earth to speak with the Wisdom Keepers and respectfully sharing what they are learning and experiencing with us, through the media, books, and workshops. Their journeys may help to re-awaken (awaken again) the seeds which already lie dormant within us.

In the end, our reality is created by the choices we make. *The actions of others are out of our control. Our reaction to them is completely our own.* There is no truth or merit in blaming society, our parents, the weather, our spouse, our former spouse, our job, our children, or any other outside factors. *We* are responsible for every one of our choices and decisions. *This fact makes us more powerful than we may think we are.*

I, like so many of us, have spent much of my life thinking I was inadequate... denying my own inner truths, feeling flawed, yet seeing a dimly lit "other" version of myself... expansive, loving, worthy, powerful, magical, dare I say... perfect. Then turning away shamefully, in the mistaken belief it was wrong! After all, who am I to think such lofty thoughts!?! Well... who am I not to?

Pow!!!
This is a book of love... of hope... of peace... of compassion. For, in *"Sharing Light"* (cover art by author), how could it be otherwise!?!

Stop. Breathe. Be. Repeat.

Amid chaos, create calm.

All is Well

dark of night is lifting

as morning breezes stir

the dreamer remains

transfixed deep inside

where past present and

all the spaces to come

weave together

in a dance of magic

too powerful

to abandon lightly

illusion falls away somehow

in this garden of the soul

all the drama and chaos

of the waking world

means nothing here

where truth is simple

and the answer

appears obvious

without fear

there is only love

all is well

The Journey: Authors' Notes

Life can be somewhat like trying to solve a crossword puzzle without any clues. As you attempt to navigate life, the ordered structure of its little boxes makes no sense. Sure, it looks great, the gleaming grid all tidily and artfully arranged. Where to start? How to go about it? An incomprehensible number of possible combinations! Can it ever sort itself out... without clues... without "suggestions" of the "right" answers?... Is this all we have? And is that okay?

Humanity is a strange species. The Spirit Self carries within it the seeds of Infinite Wisdom. It has the potential and the ability to open to All That Is, to access all of the Wisdom and Experience the Collective Realms have ever known. *Every* newborn baby comes into the world fully awake, and aware of their Divine Perfection and Purpose... *They remember everything! They know who they are, where they have been, and where they are going! It's like arriving in their tiny Earth baby bodies, with a Life Manual in hand, energetically speaking!*

It is the birthright of every child everywhere, to be magnificent, not just a few VIP's and holy sages. This message is paramount to hear, read, ponder, internalize, and accept! It is a timely reminder for every human being **right now** to take this message to heart and allow it to flower there!

There is no end to your potential. You are infinite. As I write this manuscript, I become increasingly aware of this simple, and yet profound truth. It was, is and shall always be so. It resides within us all, just beyond the veil of forgetfulness we assume/ acquire soon after we enter human form.

Encouraged and supported by parents, teachers, the media, society and religious doctrines, the veil (false-self) settles in. It is our ego-self (human persona). So, early in life, children learn to stop mentioning their magic. To please parents and others, they gradually shut down and conform to the particular "truths" they are taught.

I see the beauty and sacredness in my own precious grandchildren and in other youngsters I am blessed to encounter in my life. When they speak of their spirit friends, I do not chastise them. When they tell me they can feel energy in crystals and stones, I do not laugh at them or act uncomfortable with such talk. When they share their dreams and visions with me, I listen with respect.

I ask them to share their Truths with me in their own words. I am honored when they feel safe to do so. It is extremely important to allow children to explore their inner landscape freely and fearlessly. It will help them discover how to "be" in their outer world as well! And it is paramount, to let them share it with you, without passing any judgement! When a child experiences ridicule, disbelief and/ or other negative judgements of their unbridled sharing, they tend to feel shameful and shut down.

Recently, I was lucky enough to spend a few minutes in the company of pure magic. I met a little girl not yet six months of age, the granddaughter of a dear friend. As I chatted away with her, she held my finger in her chubby little hand. It was very apparent that she was looking deeply into my eyes, and far beyond into my Spirit. I made my energetic aura as open as I could. We remained transfixed, as she gazed beyond here into the realm of Spirit. She studied my energy field... a glimpse of curiosity, a few fleeting smiles, excitement, wide eyes. Then, when she was done, her gaze returned to my human presence in the room. And she smiled that soft, beautiful baby smile. I feel blessed by our encounter.

So, what then, is "reality"? Reality is only a self construct, a very subjective thing. It is carefully crafted by the ego-self, as it strives to make sense of the world around it. As a child learns and grows into adulthood, they do the best job possible to figure out right and wrong, real and imagined, and to sort out where they belong. In the end, it is largely an individual thing. *One does not react to "reality." One reacts to what they are, at that moment, choosing to believe about "reality."*

And so, it goes……. *"Reality"* changes from era to era, from culture to culture, from one religion or spiritual path to another, and within any given socio-economic class. We must also recognise that; *it is almost entirely based on someone else's very human thoughts and ideas!* Conventional leaders, be they political, religious, business based or otherwise, often mould the *"reality"* of their sphere of influence, through lenses that do not seek to assist and support the masses. They rather seek to augment their own power, control and riches. So, the adage that *the only thing real is illusion,* is indeed based in fact!

And yet somehow, through the ages, people have largely clung to their "place" and fulfilled their "designated role." Looking at the very words "designated role", one can easily see that <u>designed</u> and <u>assigned by society</u>, a.k.a. those in power, are the critical factors here. The idea of a great being (God) who rules "on high" and fully supports the ruling class/ king has been implemented and enforced for a long time with little room for personal growth or change in status.

Still, deep within the human heart, is the desire to strive for a connection to, and an understanding of, a Supreme Being who is the Creator and Caretaker of All That Is... of us!!! Only this, for many of us, could make sense and give purpose to the chaos and confusion of life on Mother Earth today.

I have always struggled with the word "God." The commonly accepted image of "God" is male. I do have quite a few Pagan and Wiccan friends though, who see female "Goddess" images when pondering the divine. Both may be right. Both may also be wrong!

It seems to me, that the Creator of All That Is, if you believe in such things, is neither <u>and</u> both. This Great Being does not seek to recreate itself, at least not in the ways we understand. Nor can it be some divine lord in some divine location far away, pulling our strings.

In antiquity, it was almost universally thought, that there was a Great Mother Goddess/ Creator. It made sense to folks that a female deity was in charge. After all, was it not women who brought forth new life from their bodies? Who nurtured the newborn children with milk that literally flowed from their breasts? Who cared for their families and communities when they were hungry, unwell, injured? Who taught the young the skills to survive and thrive? And so, the respectful worship of the Goddess held sway across many centuries.

But then things began to change. As the patriarchy took control, the Great Mother Goddess went deep underground into secrecy. Her kinder, gentler ways of being still survive. They are entering the mainstream more openly all the time. And She is accepted and respected more fully as we remember.

Many years ago, my master/ teacher withdrew from the room after meditation. She said that Spirit had a "journey" for me to take. I closed my eyes and opened my energy field to accept the Spirit Journey to come. I felt myself drifting away. I saw through my inner eye as I travelled through the ethers, through the clouds, past beautiful blue, indigo and purple starry spaces. I did not know where I was, but I knew I was travelling verrrrry far. And it felt awesome! …. Peace. Love. Joy….

Finally, after what seemed a very long time, I came to a space of great, floating light. Moving forward, I felt humbled, honored, and awed! All at once! As the mist cleared, I knew I was in a very auspicious place. A place of greatness.

A Being approached me, floating through the ethers. It was dressed in a light-colored robe, and held a glowing ball of light in its hands. At first, I though the Being was male, so I bowed and said, "Greetings Grandfather." Then, it seemed to be an ancient and ageless female, so I bowed and said, "Greetings Grandmother." Finally, I understood. This Great Being was neither and both, at the same time!

I was a bit confused as to why I was being gifted with a visit to this most holy place!?! The Being held out the ball of light to me, and I felt its warmth. It placed the ball of light into my heart chakra. I was amazed!!

"Child, share this Light freely with all you meet. It will grow bigger and bigger until it consumes you. You shall become that Light! It is only if you keep it to yourself, that it shall grow small and die out."

This encounter has changed my ways of being around the subject of "Divine Truth." As more and more moments unfold, in this worldly creation we call "time," my understandings unfold as well. Illusions fall away. Truth remains. Truth is as familiar as it is strange, somehow uncomfortable, and yet it fits like a well-worn glove.

I am God! You are God! Each and everything (every thing) is a spark of God/ Goddess/ Creator/ Allah, *including us*! Wow!?! Let's read that again. I am God! You are God! Nothing (no thing) is not God! It is very hard for the human brain to wrap itself around this idea! Especially after so many centuries of being told otherwise!

And yet, it is as simple as it is complex! We are each other. That which I do to you, I do to myself. The illusions of me and you, us and them, worthy and unworthy, superior and inferior are merely that… illusions! Made up stuff! They are passed down from generation to generation, as the norms and mores upon which a society is based….. truth with a small "t."

Babies know. Babies remember the ethereal spaces from whence they came. We can return to that knowing. Most of us glimpse our true state of being here and there. I am God. You are God. We are told we are made in God's image. It is more than that. We **ARE** God.

All is well… always, in all ways… even when it may not seem so from time to time! I continue to learn and grow as we all do. I have tried in my ways, to share the light by opening my heart-space to speak, to sing, to write, as much and as able ever since. And life's journey continues, one moment following the other, in an endless dance.

Nasturtiums: The Metaphor

nothing beautiful, natural, uplifting, and true
can forever be hidden from view

A dear friend of mine, is also a fabulous teacher. She is what we might call a "contrary teacher." This is someone who teaches their lessons, by stirring up your emotions enough to make you stop and (hopefully) think about your current conditioning (ego-based opinions) around a subject. In the mornings, she often accompanies me when I walk my dog. Our conversations vary day-to-day, often centering around the beauty of the natural world.

We sometimes walk by a place on the pathway, where people dump grass clippings, flowers and other things they have discarded from their gardens and lawns. My friend seems fixated on "rescuing" every single plant that even remotely seems viable, and bringing it home to replant it there. I admittedly, sometimes become a bit tired of (judgmental of) her efforts.

For a few days in a row, we noticed a little patch of brightly blooming yellow nasturtiums. Despite being ripped out and discarded, they had re-rooted themselves and were growing there amongst the plant clippings, etc. behind some tall weeds. *She was enchanted!* "Don't you see how beautiful this is!?! It's like they have always been there! I wonder if anyone else will even notice them, hidden away like that?" She fretted about it quite a bit.

Then one day, refusing to leave them there any longer, she went back out, garden trowel in hand and reclaimed them. She replanted them in a more public place, where others might see them too. Every day, she watched to see if they took root, grew, and flourished. She pointed them out to everyone who happened by. As of this writing, they remain healthy and alive! And many folks who might never have come across them, enjoy seeing the bright yellow nasturtiums in their new more visible location.

When pondering this whole little tale, I was reminded of a beloved elder's words long ago. He said that anything that is truly from Spirit will resurface when it is the right time. This dear woman saw the beauty and the value in the yellow nasturtiums, seemingly lost to the world. Gently, lovingly, she restored them to a place where they would flourish and uplift others every day! And so it is, with many hidden spiritual truths! They are re-surfacing every moment of every day! A'Ho!

Once you know something, you cannot go back and pretend you don't! When faced with several choices, none of which seem at all reasonable, or even palatable, is it ever okay not to choose? Can one simply walk away? The peril in this is that your right and ability to at least *register* your story is not exercised. There is nothing to be gained later, in judgements cast.

Yet, sometimes a respectful, considered nonaction and withdrawal is in order. That can speak volumes about your position on the matter. It avoids confrontation, conflict and/ or feeling maneuvered into choosing poorly. The energy saved is now free to do something else you are passionate about instead.

One of my favorite ways to avoid important tasks like writing, while at the same time, keeping my mind occupied, is to do endless Sudoku puzzles. (Sudoku books are readily and inexpensively available in any city or town.) Here is a bit of wisdom that I have gleaned while Sudoku puzzle solving. *If you keep at anything long enough, all the pieces fall into place. Even seemingly impossible tasks will eventually reach completion. All puzzles can be solved...*

confusions cleared... answers found. Eventually things add up. You may need to keep at it for a long time. If you set it down for a while and then come back, a clear head sees what was previously obscured. What a great feeling when you sort it all out! It was worth all the work! Whoo Hoo! You did it!

It is important to withdraw all attachment to the outcome. Every choice made, moment to moment, serves to help open and expand one's consciousness. So, there are no mistakes, just choices made. And with any luck at all, you learn from them. To quote my son on the matter; "Don't worry about it, Ma. It's all good." I will expand upon these concepts later in the book.

Learn to appreciate those who follow their own hearts regardless of what others think. For they open windows and pathways to the deepest avenues of your soul.... avenues long ago gobbed shut and overgrown with brush and weeds that somehow disguised their very existence.... as if they were never there in the first place. These now open windows and pathways are the true access to your purest self. They are eternal, godly, balanced, loving reflections of the One. They are unfettered by dogmatic rules and restrictions. They set you free...... like your free-thinking friends...... the poets, rebels and outcasts in your life.

When you view the world from the inside out, seemingly simple stuff begins to appear complex. You see the way the fabric has been cut and rejoined together, so carefully it had appeared seamless. You notice unusual patterns emerging. The folds and pleats of the hills and valleys are new and strange. The familiar is suddenly unrecognizable. Your feet slip and strain to adjust. It takes great effort to maneuver and re-establish your footing. Nothing you ever knew, nothing you ever thought you knew, is valid any longer.

What is this? Is it safe? Is it real? Are you losing it, or finding it? Is there even time to think about it? Can you act.... Or just react? Can you trust your version of God to look after you, and just be with it? Perhaps...... Why not?

Spirit (God) has a way of helping you to remember at the right speed and time. For me, it has been a process, occurring over a long period of years, since childhood...*There is a space, a pure space beyond words, where Spirit dwells.* A space where everything comes together. A space between the heartbeats. Where everything merges. And we are One. During the course of a lifetime, it is possible to reach this place sometimes, even for a few moments, and then return to your body to continue your Earth Journey. I have seen this place. I have felt it. I have breathed it in. I have been it. I am grateful and blessed. The Buddhists call it the Brahma Worlds. The Christians might call it Heaven. I cannot name it. I cannot name the un-nameable. There is no need to attach an arbitrary label to such a place. *It is more an experience than a place.*

You cannot <u>think</u> your way there, no matter how you train your brain, or what great wisdom is brimming forth from your learned mind. Getting there is actually a *"no brainer"* both literally and figuratively. So, what does that mean? It means that Utopia, Heaven, Enlightenment lies in a different locale. It is found deep within your heart. SO... you can't *<u>think</u>* your way to Nirvana. You must *<u>feel</u>* your way there. When we do that, we live as the Divine Being we truly are.... a.k.a. God......

The teachings of the Anishinaabe peoples of North America, which encompass the Ojibwe, Chippewa, Saulteaux, Oji-cree, Odawa, Potawatomi, Mississauga, Nipissing and Algonquin (Basil Johnston, Ojibwe historian) tell us that we were lovingly breathed into life from the nothingness (the ethers) a long time ago by Gitchi Manitou, the Great Spirit, who is the Creator of All Things. We were given a sacred task as "Keepers of the Earth" to be the caretakers for all of creation, and for Mother Earth Herself. But somehow, we became lost along the way. We gave our attention over to worldly pursuits and narrowed our focus to include only ourselves and our own needs/ wants.

This is a time unlike any other on our little blue planet. We are at a crossroads. The wheel is at a tipping point. *"Ye reap what ye sow."* This biblical passage certainly fits the situation we are currently in. All of the short-sighted ways humans have conducted ourselves for centuries are rearing their heads and demanding attention.... racism, genocide, elder neglect and abuse, gender inequality, family breakdown, child poverty, war, famine, corruption in politics and religious institutions, pollution, and on and on. Time has come to speak up for the ones who cannot speak for themselves!

"When the whole world is silent, even one voice becomes powerful."
.........Malala Yousafzai

Many years ago, a wise elder told me this... "And the time will come, when a new nation will arise. They will be called the Rainbow People. They will be from all races, all cultures and all paths. They will be Warriors of the Great Peace. They will remain connected to Mother Earth and to all who dwell upon Her Face. They will create and support ways of love, ways of healing the darkness and fear that is growing everywhere. The human family cannot then go backward. Or stand still. We will go forward together as ONE!" This is that time! Knowing what must take place to restore balance, we are by virtue of that awareness, a part of the process!

Piidawbin... Dawn

no longer night

not yet day

shadows lifting to expose

the beauty and the beast

and i finally see promise

instead of only pain

nothing is missing here

all is well

accepting what is

shaking hands with those gifts

which in their way imparted

the lessons i came to learn

in gratitude and humility

wounds heal

i am safe

time to stand tall

facing the unknown day

strong and whole

i am at peace

with myself

at last

"Owning our story and loving ourselves through that process is the bravest thing that we'll ever do."
...Brene Brown

I have been compelled to research my family's roots as a legacy for my children and grandchildren for an exceedingly long time. When I sent away my DNA for analysis a few years ago, my journey took me farther than I could have imagined. It has significance on a much broader scale than my immediate family and circle of friends. It could be considered insanity, blasphemy or simply read and pondered upon as presented. It has merit and is of interest, no matter your perspective on life.

Every family has secrets. Every family has controversy. Every family consists of a combination of the known and the unknown. There are the old trunks in the attic, full of mementos and antiquated photographs of people dressed in strange clothing. Folks you cannot quite recognise. Long departed relatives. Somehow, you know they are a part of you. There are the stories told by your parents, your aunts and uncles, your grandparents and other older family members. As a child, you listened politely, under your mother's watchful eye, and as soon as possible, you escaped to your room to play. A familiar tale in many homes......

But the stories, and the faces in the pictures stayed with me. They were hiding in the just-beyond-now places of my memory. As I grew up and began a life and family of my own, I wondered about those people and their lives. I became curious about the roots of my family tree. I wanted to share our heritage with my children and their children. I decided to learn more about it.

When I had my DNA tested, I expected certain things to be verified. I expected the documented results to corroborate who I always thought I was. And that did happen, to some degree. Then, digging a bit deeper, surprises emerged. Shocking surprises! One day, the Truth became undeniable. OMG! I found the word "Desposynos" (descendant of Christianity's Holy Family) and its plural "Desposyni" .... And I am that! My "real world" blew up. So, I shut down, closed myself off from everything for a while. I needed to regroup.

I double checked. I second guessed. I asked relatives what they knew about it. I became consumed with research. I poured over old church records, ancestry trails, historical anecdotes, biblical scriptures. I delighted in pictures of long deceased ancestors. I connected with cousins halfway around the world I did not even know I had. I Googled it. I shared some things with a few close friends and family members. I was on a mission to uncover everything! How could this be possible!?!.... a woman with her feet in two worlds.... Or in many!?!

If Jesus Christ has descendants (Desposyni) living in the world today, what are their lives like? Where are they living? How do they look? Would we recognize them for who they truly are? Do they recognize themselves for who they truly are? Billion-dollar questions indeed! Something most of us have never pondered upon, given the prevailing biblical claims that he never married and/ or had children. And yet, given the laws of generational expansion, there must be millions of Desposyni living in the world today, walking beside and amongst us, whether they may be consciously aware of their identity as such, or not!!

An elder once told me that anything hidden from the world, will always find the light and resurface if it is Spiritual Truth. If something is truly from Gitchi Manitou, the Creator of All That Is, it will resurface in a timely manner. This is it! Truth, as *"they"* say, is stranger than fiction. In the end, it is also much more pleasant.

"Truth" like "reality" is subjective. It varies from person to person and from group to group. It differs by religion, by culture, by socio-economic group. And even within each person's lifetime, s/he shifts their thinking about truth, as they learn, grow, and experience different events and changes. *What was "true" last year, last month or even a few moments ago, may shift dramatically in just a heartbeat.* Never more so on Mother Earth than now!

"The times, they are a' changin'." … Bob Dylan

Today, I am more aware than ever, that it is time to speak out. What is the payoff to be gained from doing nothing?... fitting in? being part of the crowd? being accepted? Staying small and silent never allows anyone to be fully free. I write this for all the kindred spirits who hold back, who fear to trust wings broken lifetimes ago. *Within the human heart, lie the keys to Love, Profound Peace and Eternity.*

The Buddha once said; "Do not accept anything as Truth just because I say it is so. Go out and examine its validity for yourself." Sage advice! Can we make peace with our own understandings. Can we respect and consider other ideas and views without great emotional distress? Let us each and all, be diligent and mindful in our search for meaning.

A "Leap of Faith" occurs when we test the parameters of our present path and know we are safe. We can experience other avenues of existence, without f.e.a.r precluding such adventures. Kind of like leaping off a cliff into the unknown, steeped in the faith that all is well. And trusting that the landing will be a good one, even if in a rocky place. Standing strong, wherever we find ourselves, and grateful we have chosen to take the journey.

Many years ago, I had such a dream. I stood on the summit of a high cliff. The spirit guide who was interacting with me simply said "Jump!" I looked down at the rocks far below and the waves crashing on the shoreline. For a moment, I hesitated, thinking what could happen. Then, trusting my guide and my path, I ran to the edge and just jumped off, in complete trust. Guess what!?! I flew! I soared over the scene below! That my friends, is a Leap of Faith!!

<u>Faith</u>

faith is the knowing

that all is well

it is that simple

stripped clean of

the dogma of religion

no rules

or regulations

there is only

the knowing that

love and truth

are one

and that is

all you need

"Leap of Faith" ... by Andrea Wolfe... c. 2016

The Angel at the Waterfall

in the presence of our lady

and her precious child

all else falls away

time and space are meaningless

reality pales and disappears into shadow

as the Blessed Angel stands softly

and allows the waterfall to continue

in its way, clearing, cleansing

falling forever

ancestral spirits appear from

within the solid rock walls

keeping watch o'er the pair

silent sentries surround

Babe clings to Mom

but he has no fear

head rests on Angel's breast

and he sighs content

she wonders if this time

they will understand

as she cradles

her most precious gift

Old Age/ New Age…. Religion to Spirituality

The concept of "i am" vs: "I AM" is not new. It has been a popular New Age concept for some years now. So, for this writing it is enough to say the following as a brief explanation. The "i am" refers to the human ego-based self. This is the way we perceive ourselves on a personal, individual, human level. When we introduce ourselves to someone, it might go something like this: "My name is…………. I am a 47-year-old teacher in a local grade school. I am married and a mother of three children" … and so on…….. The *"I AM"* refers to something much more intrinsic within us all, the *"Higher Self"* or the *"Spirit Self."* This is the *soul* part of us, eternal and ever connected to All That Is (God/ Goddess). It is not a part of any specific religion or spiritual path. It is much more than that. It is the Spark of the Divine, inherent in everyone. We will return to these concepts many times during this rewriting of history/herstory and rethinking of reality as we know it.

There have always been light-sharers. There have been poets, mystics, gurus and guides. And today, more seers are re-membering themselves (putting their whole selves back together) and awakening from their slumbering state. These are the free thinkers, who are choosing to share stories that dare to defy the *"norms "*of the societies at large within which they live. YouTube, social media, television, movies, books and other mass media methods allow world-wide access. Even those who continue to dismiss them as unworthy of merit, are still aware of them. We cannot afford to ignore these issues any longer.

We have all heard of the New Age. Who knows exactly when it began? We do know that, in the 1960's, many people became quite disillusioned with the values espoused by a society more interested in money and power than in people. The '60's were a time of such events as the Viet Nam War, the U.S. Race Riots, Woodstock and the Hippie Movement. It was a time when people, especially the youth marched, protested, carried placards and shouted such slogans as "Free Love," "Power to the People," "Make Love Not War", etc. World leaders demanded an end to the racial discrimination that kept Black Americans impoverished and disadvantaged. Dr. Martin Luther King Jr.'s "I Have a Dream" speech touched the hearts of the nation and the world deeply and profoundly, and he mobilized people to action. He became the face of the civil rights movement.

And a New Age was born! Spirituality reached the forefront, as an antidote to religion. Indigenous Peoples Spirituality and Wicca, once sanctioned and harshly repressed, resurfaced. Buddhist, Muslim, Hindu and other older Spiritual Paths took hold in the West and blossomed. People meditated, journaled, prayed and listened to new concepts and new gurus. Books hit the shelves talking about past lives, hypnotherapy, loving-kindness, forgiveness and all sorts of new ways of being. With the advent of the internet, the messages began to reach world-wide audiences in never-before-seen numbers. Inspirational speakers wrote books, made films and travelled far and wide to spread their message of "Love and Light."

Some years back, many people on the spiritual path decided that the ego is bad. There was a lot of talk about leaving the ego behind. "Check your ego at the door" and such-like. The late great Dr. Wayne W. Dyer used to say that if the **EGO** were in charge, it would **E**dge **G**od **O**ut. I don't think he meant to send our human self off to some distant planet! We need that human identity, our "mind self" if we are going to hang out in our body for any length of time. It has been given to us so our spirit self (Higher Self) can experience itself in an earthly human form. We have chosen to come here to learn earthly lessons, to assist self and others to grow lighter, and hopefully, to be kind to all, including Mother Earth.

We are no longer ignorant of what is creating chaos and thwarting peace. We can create change. When I am fully plugged into my spiritual essence, I am expansive, creative, holy and whole. I AM All That Is (God). No boundaries exist. There are no in-between spaces, no "others", only the Whole. As a human being, this is very difficult to conceptualize. As a spirit being, it's a no brainer! Literally as well as figuratively.......

As the popular adage says; "Life is a journey, not a destination." So, let's go bravely, relentlessly forward on that journey....... together... all one, not alone! Let's restore the Sacred Circle! We are now here because on a soul level, we are choosing to be a part of the *Great Awakening* needed to restore balance on Mother Earth. Through these pages, we will strive to find ways of being that will foster a return to the Light and Love lost in dark spaces centuries ago. That wise elder who told me that anything that is *Spiritual Truth* will return to the Light when it is time was right! And it is time now! May we create a *"reality"* based on the very *Spiritual Truth* we are still seeking within our inner self (heart-space).

**"You don't react to reality.
You react to what you choose to believe about reality."**

Bishop T.D. Jakes

"Allow yourself the luxury of believing in the divinity of your own soul."

Dr. Wayne W. Dyer

Seven Great Teachers

my soul has been singing its song

through the immeasurable length of time

captured within the energetic imprint that

underscores the constant ebb and flow of

the many Earth Journeys undertaken in

my quest to find that place of peace

from whence i came so long ago

gently encouraging those tools which

are always at the ready to help me heal

"Seven Great Teachers" spoken of since days of old

'love, respect, courage, honesty, humility, wisdom, truth'

the ancestors impart a code for living in good ways and

my human-ness attempts to follow their lead

letting go of the lower energies that

urge more selfish directions

to take as my path

i struggle with the task

as i settle into morning meditations

evening prayers and dream-time visions

how to return to my true and original state of being

light and love and the "Seven Great Teachers" of the ancestors

then i remember that even here in the valley of shadows

the darkest most fearful of all places are illuminated

by a small and unassuming ray of light

that grows to guide my journey

home to myself

Remembering Me - The Family Tree

"Bless our ancestors' ancestors,

the roots of our family tree,

And bless our children's children,

the fruit that's yet to be."

- old Celtic Prayer

"Grandmother, all your tattoos are colorful and stuff. And, they're really pretty. But......."

(pause)..... continues

"When you leave your body and it turns to dust, will it be rainbow-colored dust?"

(long pause) .... smiles and answers self

"Oh, yes it will! And it is only then, that people will see how very beautiful you really are!"

...... wisdom from a 6-year-old

Sarah Mary Star

the woman who stands before you

is proud… and humble

she opens her eyes and her heart

the curtain falls and she remains steadfast

the idea of hiding seems a thing of a distant past

shrouded in the mystery of history

she is naked Truth personified

some avert their eyes

it's all too much…

bound by fear and shame

they will not dare to do the same

they judge her openness and transparency as madness

seeing no beauty in her act of love

they refuse to meet her gaze

for they are afraid it may highlight

the self deception of the illusion even further

and blow their cover all to hell

leaving in its wake an uncomfortable emptiness

a hollow space not easy to fill

Nature vs: Nurture......

A little bit of all our ancestors lives in us. *Their DNA is our DNA.* We are a crowded house. We inherit all of the magic and all of the mayhem. Things run in families. Things like hair, eye and skin color. Things like music or art talents. Like belonging to a certain social class or caste. Like stories and secrets.

And beyond all of that... the genetic imprints of ancestors crying out to be recognized, to be heard... their unresolved issues intact. Beings whose lives ended long ago. Imprints of their lifeblood flows in our veins.

Tuning in, in quiet times, I hear their call. I feel their joys and sorrows, their anguish and their urgency. Sometimes, I even catch a glimpse of them in my inner eye... in meditations and dreams... and in waking times, if my mind is still. It isn't really new for me. It has always been like this, since the awkward days of childhood.

I was born into an outwardly unremarkable lower middle-class family, the second of four children. My father worked outside the home and my mother was a home-maker (housewife), as was the custom for most married women at that time. My parents were children of the *"Great Depression"* and higher education was prized. It had been financially out of their grasp in their own youth. Our family income was small, yet we never lacked for anything we needed. I now understand, that my parents did without many things, to provide for their children. I am more grateful for their unconditional love and support than I likely told them then.

I always had my own world view. Many children do. Being wyrd (old Celtic spelling) always did have its perks. You could just be in the moment. You never knew when it would be a soft cloud, when it would be a secret fort, or even a river bank. When I was a little child, I lived in a world of magic. This kept life very interesting.

My closest friend lived nearby. We created magic kingdoms in the bush, filled with castles, kings and queens... a.k.a. tree forts, a few pet cats and other kids. We held great feasts (picnics) and invited very important and powerful rulers from far away (our parents) to share the bounty. My Dad picked wild berries with us and taught us about the gifts of nature. Our summer days were full of adventures.

I had dreams that seemed like memories. They were of other times and places far away. I began to dream sequential dreams and couldn't wait until bed-time to see the "next chapter" unfold. I started writing poetry at an early age. Because I was considered bright by the teachers at school, I was pushed ahead a couple of grades. Classmates were older and more socially advanced than I was. Their interests were not mine. I was not popular with the "in crowd." That was okay, because I was happier in my own ways of be-ing anyway.....

I spent a lot of time at home alone, as the years passed. I read books. I wrote poetry and journaled my feelings. I always knew *"they"* (spirit beings) were around me. I imagined flying above the trees. I remembered being other people, in other times and lives. I have always been a dreamer, a seer and an intuitive. That is okay. All things we encounter and the experiences we have/ create, are teachers that shape our version of reality, and how we understand things. As with most kids, I was lonely sometimes. No matter what, I always knew my family loved me. And that is an important gift. One that I hope I have since shared with my own children and their families.

I have been blessed to learn and grow in many paths and cultural beliefs. They come from all directions in the spiritual hoop, including Christianity, the Red Path (traditional Indigenous Path), Buddhism, Wicca, Hinduism, Huna Kane and New Age traditions. They will appear here and there in the pages of this book They have enhanced my journey of awakening and remembering to a great degree. To honor the sacredness of the ceremonies and events, I do not elaborate on the intimate details herein.

My family has been present here upon Mother Earth for many thousands of years. We came here from the *Star Realms* long ago. Our mission was one of Peace and Love. We walked in Atlantis and Lemuria and many ancient places. We chose to come here to assist humans to evolve and advance in their ways of being. Some early visits are documented and traceable, some are not, excepting in dreams and "spirit memories."

I am Sarah Mary Star. I am the 51st great granddaughter of Yeshua ben (son of) Youssef (Jesus Christ) and his beloved wife Maria bint (daughter of) Matthew Matteus a.k.a. Mary Magdalene. *Adam and Eve, my 96th great grandparents were not the first Earth people. Rather, they are the first star being ancestors to be well documented.* Many others followed over the centuries, settling in various locations around the planet. They brought new and advanced concepts, ideas and technology with them. Some are lost in antiquity. Many grace historical books, legends and folklore. I tell my story as accurately as my research, family stories, dreams and visions allow. And the reader may draw their own conclusions.

I shall follow the course of history over the last six thousand years or so, through the genetic trail of my family, a microcosm if you will, for the larger picture or macrocosm of Planet Earth. I use the term *"Mother Earth"* in this writing. Upon Her valleys, hills, rivers and streams, we dwell. It is this living Gaia who gives life, sustains life and provides a final resting place for our human body, when our spirit leaves it behind, during the transition we call death.

Expand your notions of us and them, of class, creed, culture, of what is important or otherwise. Know these traits dwell within all of us. The picture I paint is of my own heart and of my genetic coding. It contains some people remembered as holy, some as horrible, some as sinners, some as saints, some as concubines and some as conquerors. Each and all of my ancestors played their roles in the best ways they could, moment to moment, given the tools and understandings they had. As do all of us......

It is paramount to the advancement of the human species that, we at last choose to rebalance the patriarchal planet that we live on. It all began centuries ago, when men became the holders of power, the lawmakers, the enforcers and the rulers. Previous to that, the Creator/ Goddess face of the divine held sway quite widely.

Men were the warriors in most societies. They were physically bigger, stronger and more muscular than their female counterparts. Nor were they tied down by the tasks naturally assigned to women, of multiple pregnancies, and the nurturing of many children. These things left women vulnerable and dependant upon their mates for food, protection, and safety for themselves and their children.

Today, even with our vast stores of knowledge, advancements in technology, smaller families to care for, and access to higher education for women, the patriarchy persists. This limits the growth and evolvement of our species greatly. It is only with the restoration of women to their rightful place, as equal partners beside men in all areas of life, that we shall ever grow towards our full potential... "history" (his story) and "herstory" (her story) told together, weave a tapestry that is in essence, *"ourstory" (our story).*

Looking at all the various versions of things, the tale told herein, is much more balanced, much more congruent, and much more user friendly. As never before, increasing numbers of books, speakers and mass media methods are emerging that are retelling biblical and religious tales and cultural folklore/ legends differently. They reach us through revealing long hidden manuscripts, through channelled information from spiritual ancestors and through a massive undertaking into genetic research. I recommend accessing some of this material yourself, if you wish. There are many excellent sources of information available for the seeker.

After a very long time of researching the ins and outs of my family tree, patterns emerged, hidden in plain sight. Over the centuries, coinciding with times of war and great social unrest, the family tree branches seem to intertwine. It is as though, the ancestors somehow relied upon the bloodlines re-merging, to strengthen their genetic and human influences in times of chaos. Many examples abound.

Most recently, the Desposynic bloodlines of my maternal grandparents merged in the 1900's to create my mother and her siblings. Both were descendants of Yeshua (Jesus) and Maria Magdalena. Their lines have come down through the ages, melding here and there. They were notably connected through the Royal Stewarts in the 1300-1400's. And then, they diverged for the most part for several centuries, still intermarrying here and there, as royal families tend to do. It seems a timely joining of these two branches of the clan, after all that these modern times are bringing forth.

The seers predict that it is paramount to make great changes in order to continue living here, on "our little blue planet, third from the sun." There are hundreds, perhaps thousands of posts daily on social media, interspersed with the Covid-19 data (case counts, deaths, vaccines) … about pollution, global warming, disappearing species, famine, religious intolerance, wars, child abuse, animal abuse, racism, corrupt politicians, genocide, Monsanto, and on and on. If we choose to, we can spend hours each day, immersed in negative news stories. We think we are "helping" when we click sad face emojis, angry face emojis, or like emojis, depending on the slant of the story. We repost them, so everyone else can read the story and click their emojis. Hours may slip by, with all of our energy focused on horrible, violent and unacceptable data. Time to simply **stop it**!

Many folks are addicted to the endless beeps, alarms and rings that alert them to whatever technological devices they have at the ready. During a family get-together some time ago (before Covid-19), after not seeing each other for over a year, everyone's phones beeped every few minutes with weather reports, even though we weren't going anywhere. If a topic was being discussed, at least a few would Google it for more information. The television went on at every newscast. No one spoke during it. And so on. As the only one without a cell phone, I spent a lot of time in silence, petting the cat.

Adding Covid-19 and the extremes of the current world upheaval to this mix, we can get a pretty clear picture of today's atmosphere. We have chosen to be here now and have the right and the ability to uplift ourselves and our lives, which will help Mother Earth to heal and be strong. This must be done in loving and peaceful ways.

Mother Teresa once refused to participate in an "anti-war rally" and told the surprised organizers she would never participate in an anti-war rally! She told them that, should they ever organize a "pro-peace rally", she would be honored to attend…… Wherever we place our attention is more powerful than we may realize! We create what we focus upon. A self-fulfilling prophecy, we can call it. "Thoughts become things… choose the good ones." …we are reminded by author and public speaker Mike Dooley (tut.com)

When I studied with the Anishinaabe elders, they told me that the Creator had placed small groups of *Star Beings* in many places around the planet, so that the *Star Teachings* would reach many ears when the time was right. *This IS the time long prophesied by the seers and sages of many nations!* This is the time to make momentous changes in gentle and nurturing ways! *We are the ones we have been waiting for!* Without further ado, I will take the reader on a journey through time and space, through many centuries and many cultures. These are the paths taken by my ancestors and yours to bring us here to this exact moment.

I have drawn from sources such as religious and historical records, elders' teachings, genetic analysis, Wikipedia, and many other books and manuscripts. Most of you are familiar with at least some of this material. I have also added relevant knowledge and understanding from dreams, visions, ceremony and meditation. It is important to understand who we truly are as the human family, and what we can create here.

Old rules and mores have and are breaking down in today's chaotic world. We try to steer the course of our lives in turbulent waters, with no clear direction…. and no oars. When you take away a person's oars, the boat doesn't know where to go. It rocks aimlessly about in life's ocean. The waves are so high and ominous, they threaten to crush it. Like the little popsicle stick boats we built as kids, with only flour and water paste to hold them together. These lovingly created craft always seemed to come apart the first time we launched them in the bathtub ocean. And the sturdy crew of Lego sailors were invariably doomed to be lost at sea.

By the time we reached adulthood, most of us had adopted a way of being that served as oars to steer the course of our life. By and large, it was based on the spiritual path we learned as children, our level of understanding, and the laws and ideals of the society within which we live. Our media exposure encroaches upon us, like foggy patches along the shoreline. There are always sudden shafts of sunlight, bursting through the fog. These are gifts of Spirit. They color our world and bathe us in insight. And we shine forth, at least for a while.

A great spiritual teacher of mine, and I suspect many of you, is the late Dr. Wayne W. Dyer. He used to remind us, that the opposite of "love" is not "hate." It is **FEAR**…. **F**alse **E**vidence **A**ppearing **R**eal. Hate is merely one of the many faces of fear. When I experience negative emotions like anger, hatred, judgement, and such-like, regarding someone or something, it is because I am afraid. I dig in my heels and make the other person or people wrong. Then, I can feel quite justified in my own self-righteous condemnation of them. Much easier than admitting to myself, that *I am "choosing" these negative feelings. No one is "causing" them.* Rather, they are my reaction to outer circumstances. *This is a big deal! A light bulb moment!*

It's scary when you realize you are sitting in the soup of your own sh**. "OMG! This isn't the Love and Light of Transcendence I was just meditating on!" In fact, it's pretty damned unpleasant to say the least! This is not where/ how I want to be. Time to change things. Time to let go of the "sludge" of blaming others for my current sadness, anger, imbalance, and all the other "poor me/ poor us" victim thinking. Past events are just that, past. *The done cannot be undone.*

The elders always say that this is a planet of free will. And so, every moment of every day, we get to choose how to feel, what to do and what truths to hold as dear and right.

Sometimes, we choose wisely. Sometimes, we don't. However, by shedding a clear light on what has been, we can learn from the past, and create a much kinder and more loving present and future.

It is said that we are more alike than different. There has long been the Nature vs. Nurture argument regarding how we are, at this moment, living our lives. Lately, many of us are giving merit to the idea that ancestral influences have had a lot to do with shaping our lives. It is that very thing that caused me to delve into my own genetic background, and eventually to write the words you are reading right now.

There are television shows on the subject such as "Finding Your Roots" and "Who Do You Think You Are?" Both acclaimed series help many of our popular celebrities explore their ancestral backgrounds. Some of their genetic trails lead to surprising historical places. And we are hooked!

So, many of us "regular folks" are sending off our own DNA samples to one of the myriads of companies that are springing up everywhere, to be analyzed. Some of these companies have been touted as more reputable than others. I chose a large, respected, world-renowned company for my journey of discovery. They are one of the first genetic research firms, one of the largest, and have a vast data base. I felt that working with them would create credibility and a wider scope of records, information and a family tree with many branches. That sure proved to be accurate.

Without the DNA analysis, I would have pieced together part of the picture. No doubt, I would have filled in a few blanks and thought I was "done." However, the more I researched my family tree, the more complex its branches. The farther-reaching its scope. The more intriguing its significance to *history*, and more pointedly, to *ourstory*. My ancestors wove their seed and their story back and forth through the ages, through many cultures and societies on many world stages, allowing them to influence and help to shape our modern world. They began with peaceful and lofty goals. Some they have accomplished. Many they have not yet brought to fruition. And so, we their descendants continue the work. As we awaken, so we move forward.

The "bigger picture" is very big indeed. People are beginning to question long-accepted versions of "truth". More and more people are studying and reporting on inconsistencies and falsehoods in biblical scriptures and other respected writings. The real stories are re-emerging from places they were hidden for safe-keeping long ago. Folks are finally grasping the extent of human interference… the power struggles, the violence, the lies and corruption. "Sacred" stories are often no longer sacred. We are flooded with media of all kinds, and from all perspectives, on spirituality, religion and any other subject we wish to learn about. It is good.

"Truth" must resonate deeply and *feel* right, or it is time to question it. In today's world, there is no end to resources. Information abounds to satisfy the enquiring mind and the longing heart. It is not by accident that you have been drawn to this book. Enjoy reading the material presented herein. Research its concepts if you want to. Just Google it! Or YouTube it! Read it! Write it! As in all things, take the best and leave the rest.

If I stand here, as a direct descendant of the "holy family", I should have this aced, right? If the same DNA that coursed through the veins of Mary, Youssef and their son Yeshua is within me, shouldn't I be beyond negative emotions? I wish this were true. Surely, I do. The truth is, I struggle with these things, as did they, as do we all.

In any case, this little poem holds a pearl of timeless wisdom suitable for all of us.

Touch

moving through life
the most powerful thing
is to touch even one other
living being
with love

that simple act will
reverberate endlessly outward
and change everything
forever

FREEDOM

Fearlessly

Radiating

Ever

Expanding

Degrees

Of

Magic

The Family Saga:

Step One: "The Great Plan"

Today, spiritual speakers, workshops, the internet, books and social media are awash with tales of the Interplanetary Galactic Council, light language, the akashic records, earthbound avatars, alien visitors, spiritual downloading and much more. A day does not pass without something catching the seeker's eye on at least some of these topics. There is very little truth in some tales, some truth in many tales, and much confusion in general, regarding their "reality." In the end, each of us must choose what, if any of these claims we will give credibility to. It is challenging, given the great variety of religious, spiritual, cultural, political and other societal norms, that are blended into the mixture. This is my own version of things, told in my own way.

I have had first hand knowledge of the Interplanetary Galactic Council (Star Council of Elders) for a very long time. It is only in the last few years, that I have become aware others do as well. Every so often, I have been *"called"* there in my meditation or in dream-time. The first time I can consciously recall going there, many years ago, I felt very small and a bit uncertain why I was there. I hung my head in respect and concern. Did I do something wrong? Who were they? Why was I there? I knew it was somewhere very auspicious, and that the star beings sitting around the table were pretty important and evolved. They were of many races and from many star nations. All seemed to have great light emanating from them.

We communicated without speaking, as if by telepathy. I was humbled, honored and at peace in that sacred realm. Much information was exchanged and much knowledge was passed to me, knowledge of my Earth Journey tasks and agendas. It was like a check-in, a reboot and a downloading of Star Knowledge all at once. I felt a strong kin connection with them. When it was done, they faded away, and I returned to myself, falling off to sleep in a soft mist. There have been many other visits to the Star Council of Elders in the years since that first time. And there were many others in earlier times, and in other ways, as a child...

Many millennia ago, the Interplanetary Galactic Council (Star Council of Elders) held countless meetings. The topic was a familiar one to be sure. What were the ways star beings from all nations, places and planets could work together, to assist those who inhabited Planet Earth? What could be done to facilitate a move away from the darkness (fear) that permeated their existence, causing them so much pain and suffering? How could the people living upon Planet Earth be guided toward more peaceful and compassionate ways of being? After a very long time spent in studying humanity, and consultation amongst the Star Elders, it was decided that the best way to help, was for some of them to volunteer to incarnate on Planet Earth. That way, it was assumed that the Earth people would soon open their hearts and minds to the gentle and peaceful energies presented, letting go of their less lofty, aggressive ways. And so, the *"Great Plan"* was adopted by the Council, and many star people from various star nations chose to be an active part of it. My familial ancestors were amongst them. Our journey has never been the same since. "Home" seems far away, and it is.

Some material may be new to the reader. Much has already been introduced to the public by many learned, respected and credible folks who, like myself, know it is timely to do so. Never has it been so vital to our very survival.

Step Two: Settling In: The Garden of Eden

And so, we begin with my 96th great grandparents. They were called Adam and Eve in the biblical accounts. They arrived on this planet about six thousand years ago from far away. The others who lived there at the time, were still-primitive, nomadic, hunter-gatherers, who fought amongst themselves over food, and to gain control of resources such as prime watering holes and hunting grounds. They followed the migratory patterns of the deer and antelope, dining on their meat, and some known berries and herbs.

Rumors were afoot, of a strange light in the night sky. Some were afraid. Some did not believe. Most were curious. Despite their rather exciting entrance, the newcomers were not received favorably by the people already living there. It is said in some writings, that concern and negativity may have been generated, as Adam and Eve's more permanent home base and management of the fertile valley's animals and plants was noticed. This flew in the face of the customs and ways of life the hunter-gatherers had established long ago.

Who were these strange ones? They dressed in odd clothing. Their language was unfamiliar to the ear. They built dwellings and planted things. They tended herds of animals, who somehow stayed nearby and didn't wander away. It had never occurred to anyone that animals could be kept in one place. Or that sheltering structures might be built for them in case of stormy weather. And it was also rumored that these newcomers didn't even eat meat!?! Ridiculous!! It didn't make any sense. This was not the way of things! This was not the way it was done! No, these newcomers and their odd ways were not welcome! Not at all!

And so, it was. At first, the newcomers stayed to themselves, living in peace. They had not come to cause distress. Adam and Eve anchored very high vibrational energies in their new home. Everything there flourished at the highest levels possible…. the people, the animals and the lush plant-life. The land was richly fertile. It bore fruit and other foods that provided all that they would ever need to survive and thrive. And so, they remained there happily, sustaining themselves on the abundance before them. This lush valley is now known as the "Garden of Eden," and is located in the land later to be called Israel. It is well documented in biblical and other writings.

It is recorded that Adam-First Man was born in 4004 B.C. He lived until 3070 B.C., which is a lifespan of 934 years. His wife was Eve-First Woman. Her lifespan of 926 years, was recorded as from 4000-3074 B.C.

It is variously put forth in scriptures and other writings, that they arrived on Earth as adults, "placed" there by God, or that Adam, once created, was lonely, so God fashioned Eve from a piece of Adam's rib to be his companion. Both theories have been highly and widely regarded as truth by many millions of people around the globe for millennia. Especially favored is the "Adam's Rib" theory.

*** *The word (originally found in the Sumerian language) commonly translated as "rib", can also be translated as "Favored by God" and/or as "Mother of All" …. a.k.a. "First Woman."* ***

Recall the previous story of The Star Council of Elders (Intergalactic Star Council) who had been working on the *Great Plan* to bring Planet Earth a much-needed push forward in knowledge and spiritual growth. Adam and Eve were beginning emissaries who arrived from extraterrestrial sources.

Time in the beautiful Garden of Eden grew longer. Adam and Eve had many children. They thrived and grew strong. *All of them lived lives spanning many centuries, unheard of in modern times.* It is not uncommon in the star realms, for beings to live these lengthy lifetimes. These advanced civilizations have eradicated the diseases and other threats such as war and famine that still plague us here upon Mother Earth. They are in harmony with self, with each other and with their environment. Therefore, they do not tend to age and die as we do.

The Book of Genesis says that there were two very special trees in the Garden of Eden, placed by God. One was the *Tree of Eternal Life* and the other was the *Tree of Good and Evil*. He told Adam one day, that they could eat from the Tree of Eternal Life any time. However, it was forbidden to eat from the other tree. One day, they chose to disobey God, and eat the forbidden fruit. The snake, so we are told, via the biblical account, tempted Eve. (In her defence, according to some biblical scholars, she wasn't even there when God told Adam it was off limits.) Anyway, they ate the fruit and lost the gift of eternal life granted by the other tree.

Now, let's look at this story as a <u>metaphor</u>, rather than a literal Tale of Two Trees. These star beings arrived on earth in a very high vibratory or awakened state. And so, if they stayed that way, they could live a very long time, perhaps forever. Mother Earth is a planet of free will! *Consider the Tree of Good and Evil as a metaphor for "doing the wrong thing."* When we do wrong action, we engender karma, spiritual debt. This lowers our vibratory rate, which slows us down. *So, perhaps it was more an admonishment to live in Love and Light, not breaking the rules of Good (God).*

Much discourse and speculation are given to exactly what that *"forbidden fruit"* was. When I was a child, I asked my mother. In a rather embarrassed and whispered answer, she told me it was an apple. I could not, for the life of me, figure out why an apple could cause such a stir! Later, I found that she ascribed to the notion of Eve as temptress, urging the poor and innocent Adam into a sexual act. It does seem to me that particular *"sin"* would be necessary, if God wanted them to *be fruitful and multiply* as per the Book of Genesis. So, if the *"sin"* was sex, it was not a sin at all.

More than likely, the *"forbidden fruit"* in question had to do with other things. A theory I have come across is that it encompassed the animosity the other inhabitants of the area felt, because of the disparity between the old ways of the hunter-gatherers and the staying put settlement ways of the newcomers. That does make sense. Discord lowers the energetic levels.

There is some record of another wife or consort of Adam, named Lilith Nergal. This has always been denied by biblical scholars. But the notion has persisted for all this time and deserves to be mentioned here. She is purported to have had a child together with Adam, who was named Awan bint (daughter of) Adam. Awan was born in 3895 B.C. Lilith was written about as equal to Adam in power, influence and abilities. I leave it to the reader to look for records of Lilith and/ or to rethink their understanding of Eve as "Mother of All" ….. if it feels right to do so.

In any case, it is my opinion, that the Great Mother Goddess must be restored to Her rightful place as Creator, Nurturer, Death Maven, and Rebirther, in order to restore balance and healing to Mother Earth.

Step Three: The Early Generations

Adam and Eve's son Seth lived from 3903 B.C. to 2933 B.C., a period of 970 years. He is called the *Second Patriarch.* His sister/ wife Azura Akila, *The Second Matriarch*, was born in 3874 B.C. and died in 2962 B.C. at the age of 912 years. It was considered vital to marry within the star people group and initially that meant brother-sister marriages were common/ necessary. As the centuries continue to unfold, we will look at interactions and intermarriages with others.

Seth and Azura also bore many children during their very long lives. Their son Enos was called the *Third Patriarch.* He lived from 3765 B.C. to 2860 B.C., a period of 905 years. He married his sister Noam, whose life spanned from 3765 B.C. to 2865 B.C. (900 years). Noam was the *Third Matriarch.*

Their son Canaan (Kenan) was *the Fourth Patriarch. His life spanned from 3679 B.C. to 1235 B.C.,* 1010 years, **even longer than Methuselah!!** His sister/ wife Mualeth, the *Fourth Matriarch*, lived from 3769 B.C. to 3673 B.C. *** *A life-span of only 96 years, which in present times, would be considered a good long life, was very unusual for this family at that time.* *** It is not recorded whether she suffered some mishap, left her homeland, or died of natural causes. I, for one, would be interested in this bit of herstory, currently lost in the annuls of time, as far as I know. One day, the knowledge may resurface.

Canaan and Mualeth bore a son called Mahalalel (Fifth Patriarch). His wife was his first cousin, Dina Sina (Fifth Matriarch), daughter of Barakiel (his father's brother). Their son Jared (Sixth Patriarch) and his wife Baraka, daughter of Rashujal (Sixth Matriarch) bore a son, Enoch, who is well remembered in ancient texts. Many stories exist of Enoch's life and times. He is written into scripture as a very just, kind and wise man, so beloved of God that he "was taken up to heaven in a cloud of smoke." Enoch also wrote his own detailed manuscript documenting his life and times. Many biblical references refer to knowledge of this manuscript, yet it's content was excluded from scripture.

Truth is, at that time, the people including Enoch, worshipped an Assyrian Goddess named Asherah. She was the Mother/ Creator/ Sustainer of All of Creation. Her worship and influence spread to include the land of Canaan and beyond. There were many stone and silver carvings, as well as wooden renderings. *"Asherah Poles"* stood all over Canaan and beyond, at sacred sites, for her worship.

Enoch is noted and notable for two rather exciting things! Firstly, his way of leaving his earthly life. It is written in the scriptures, Genesis 5:23, that "all the days of Enoch were three hundred and sixty-five years." It goes on to say in Hebrews 11:5-6 that "by faith Enoch was taken from this life, so that *he did not experience death*: he could not be found because God had taken him away." There are many accounts in various writings, of witnesses who saw him disappear in flames or in a puff of smoke. In modern times, many of us who have followed a spiritual path of any duration, or even those who have read rogue science novels, have heard the phrase, *"spontaneous combustion"* to describe such an event. It is usually ascribed to someone of great spiritual advancement. There are other accounts of spiritual elders who have simply disappeared in a cloud of smoke and/ or flames. The term was coined to describe such an unexplainable or *"magical"* leaving from the earth plane. And so, it was with Enoch.

The second rather noteworthy legacy of this Old Testament prophet is the following. It is widely believed in biblical and other circles, that there are only two of all the archangels, that have *ever* been in human form. All the others have always been heavenly or other-worldly beings. One of these is Metatron. Enoch is reported in the scriptures and other sources to be Metatron, so loved by God that he became an archangel when he left the earthly realms. I heard of this belief many years ago, through a teacher of mine, who could better be described as a "New Ager" rather than a Christian.

I have often encountered Metatron's spirit essence in meditations and/ or healing ceremonies over the years. He has assisted me in my own humble healing work many times. As well, Enoch the Grandfather has brought me comfort and healing many times, as I have and do cope with loss and grieving. I did not know until more recently, that we were genetically related. As they say; *"Truth is stranger than fiction."*

The children of Enoch and Edna included *Methuselah*, widely known for his very long life. I remember stories told when I was a kid about this prophet. My Mom would say; "Oh so-and-so, he's as old as Methuselah." Or, "Today I feel as old as Methuselah." As it happens, he did live a long time, with a lifespan of 946 years. He was not the longest liver in the Old Testament though. That, as near as my research indicates, was Canaan (Kenan), *(the Fourth Patriarch)*, whom we have already encountered. *His lifespan is recorded at 1010 years!* Astounding by any earthly standards to be sure!

Methuselah's son Lamech married his 1st cousin Edna, daughter of Azrail. Their son Noah is well remembered and venerated by Christians and Jews alike. Even non-secular people know the story of Noah's Ark. It is a favorite tale around the globe to this day. Noah and his wife Miriam lived prominent and prosperous lives. What you may not know about their lives, is verified in the *Scroll of Jasher*, written by someone who was a part of it. To put things in perspective, Jasher was Noah's staff bearer. So, he was privy to, in person, and at the forefront of the true story.

How do we know the Scroll of Jasher ever existed, and what it said? Because it is still in existence today! It resurfaced during the time of Emperor Charlemagne, and was the pride of his court. It is a nine-foot Hebrew scroll and has been authenticated as the real thing. *The University of Paris was founded in the year 800, specifically to translate the Scroll of Jasher!* The biblical books of Joshua and 2nd Samuel both refer to this ancient scroll, if not its contents. It confirms that women were considered equal to their male counterparts, by the Jews of that era. Their deity was the Goddess Asherah. (Remember, we talked about Asherah in the time of Enoch.) The spiritual leaders were mostly female! And Miriam was a powerful priestess with many gifts. She lived from 2450-1930 B.C., a lifespan of 520 years.

It was in fact not Noah, but Miriam who engineered the building and construction of the famous ark, "Noah's Ark!" Noah did not possess the skills, knowledge and/ or ability to conceive of the plan to build it, much less to carry it out! This did not sit well with Noah's ego image! Miriam, a powerful, shamanic, highly intelligent and capable woman was his wife, and the mother of his children. She was also a perceived threat to his masculine vision of dominance. He felt so threatened, he had her imprisoned! The Jewish people were angry with Noah for this action on his part. They rose up and set Miriam free. This retelling of the story is in the Scroll of Jasher. And Jasher was there!

The Old Testament of the Christian Bible records the children of Noah and Miriam. Three of their sons assumed great importance. Their true identities are hinted at in the scriptures, but not written about in any detail. This is where Greek, Judaic, Egyptian and other lineages merge to create magical, spiritual "myths" that have and do sustain the spirituality, if not the religiosity of many cultures and peoples of the world. The truth is written and available, as it has been for centuries. Sacred scripts say; *"for those who have eyes to see and ears to hear..."*

*** *And, they are all genetically tied to Youssef and Mary, parents of Yeshua and to Mary Magdalene, Yeshua's wife!!!* ***

I will begin with Japheth ben Noah. He is variously recorded as Yaphetidy, Yabet, Japhet and Adanya. He is called Prajapati in the writings of India. Japheth is also recorded as "the Progenitor of Europe and Central Asia." Perhaps even more significant are the names *Jupiter* and *Zeus* of Greek Olympian Titan "mythology." As it happens, he was a real man!!! And mentioned historically in the annuls of Judeo-Christian (Old Testament), Greek and Indian folklore. His lifespan, according to the Old Testament was from 2452 B.C. to 1846 B.C. or 606 years. His wife, and the mother of his children is recorded as Adatoneses bint Eliakim.

Next, we look at Shem ben Noah. He was also called Melchizedek, the "Great High Priest of Shulon." He was "The 4th Prophet of the Seal." His name is derived from the Aramaic root word **"shm"** which translates as that **"which rises and shines in space."** Christian scriptures place his lifespan as from 2454 B.C. to 1854 B.C., a period of 600 years. This is a very similar lifetime to his brother Japheth and also his brother Ham, whom we have not met yet. This is recorded in Genesis 11:10-26 and Chronicles 1:24-27. Shem's wife is Sedequelebab daughter of Eliakim, a sister of Japheth's wife Adatoneses. She lived from 2440 B.C. to 1850 B.C. (490 years). They had many children in their long lives. Their son Elam was born in 2343 B.C. Their daughter Rasueja/ Rasu'eya would later become the wife of her cousin Cush, son of Ham, whom we will meet soon.

Many of you who have followed spiritual things, will already be aware of the Order of Melchizedek and its significance. This is an ancient Spiritual Order of great honor and respect. And it is a star-based Order. This has also been known for a very long time. Again… *it is an ancient, well-respected star-based Spiritual Order.* Later, King Solomon spoke of an encounter in his time with a "very strange man" he met who was called Melchizedek, and was very wise. He said this man must have come from very far away, even farther than Canaan, because his features and manner of dress was quite unusual.

Ham is the third son of Miriam and Noah we shall mention. He is called "The Progenitor of Africa." In the book of Genesis 5:32 his lifespan is recorded as being from 2448 B.C. to 1846 B.C., a period of 602 years.

Ham's son Cush lived, according to scripture from 2200 B.C. to 2127 B.C., a much shorter time than his father and his uncles. He is also variously recorded as Chus (Black) Chaos, and Zoroaster, the "Living Star." In Chinese folklore he is called Chusou. He is remembered as a great teacher and avatar around the globe. *Zoroastrianism is a widely respected religion, which is active to this day.* His wife was Rasueja/ Rasu'eya, the daughter of Elam, the son of his Uncle Shem, as previously mentioned.

Their daughter Azurad is remembered in scripture as the wife of Eber, and the mother of King Peleg. Another daughter, Canaan is also recorded as "Niagal the Moon Goddess" from Greek Olympian fame. She married her brother Ishtar and bore his daughter Hept.

Cush and Rasueja's son Nimrod (Judaic)/ Nebrod (Greek) was the King of Assyria and Babylon. His kingdom also included Erech and Akkad, Calneh and Shinar (Sumer) according to Genesis. He was called The Mighty Hunter, Seddiya, and Ampaphel. He lived in the early Bronze Age, historically speaking. His story is recorded not only in the Bible, but in the Talmud and later in early Judaic sources (Midrash). The Book of Jubilees says he was the father of Azurad, wife of Eber and therefore, grandfather of King Peleg. He and his father talked of a One World Divinity that encompasses everything and is present here on Earth.

Nimrod began to build a great tower in Babylon, in case there was another flood, as there had been in the time of his grandparents, Noah and Miriam. This would protect the people from drowning, as so many had the last time. If there ever was another flood, the people could climb the tall tower to safety. Seems like a good idea!?!

Genesis relates the story of the Tower of Babel. We are told *"The One True God"* wanted to punish the king for trying to build a tower high enough to get *all the way up to him* (as if *God* was somewhere far away in the clouds). So, he punished poor Nimrod, and all of humanity henceforth, by creating a diverse number of languages, so people could no longer understand each other.

When people live far apart in isolated local areas, they tend to develop their own dialects and language structures, distinctive to their own group. This is a normal thing. The differences in languages already existed long before Nimrod ever tried to protect his people by building the infamous "Tower of Babel." This story has persisted though. Even today, in common usage the world over, any time a speaker is not being understood, people say they are babbling.

*** ***There is one thing that I know for sure!!! There was never, at any time, in any place, a vindictive punishing god of any sort, worshipped or otherwise!*** ***

Another son of Ham is Mizraim/ Mitzraim. He is also called Zeus, the Greek God of Lightening and Osyrus Egyptus, the 1st Pharaoh of the Zoanite Dynasty. His wife is his sister Isis, Goddess of Egypt. These three brothers and their families are significant in the cultures of Jewish, Greek, Egyptian, African and other ancient peoples.

The generations continued, and most are recorded in the Old Testament of the Christian Bible. Abraham's son Isaac is well and fondly remembered. His name translates to "Laughter" which may be a reflection of his temperament and character. Isaac's grandson Judah, son of Jacob and Leah (Rachael) bint Laban is of note. Like Mizraim, he is sometimes called Zeus and like Japheth, he is sometimes called Jupiter. These names tie he and his ancestors (and descendants) to the Greek Gods of Olympus. He is recorded in the scriptures as "the First Jew," quite a lofty title, and lived from 1753-1693 B.C. a much shorter life span than most family members at that time. He is also in the ancestral trees of Mary Magdalene, Mother Mary and Youssef, father of Yeshua.

Judah/ Jupiter/ Zeus's great grandson, Ram/ Aram is of great interest as well. His wife was none other than Kiya Tasherit, daughter of Egyptian Pharaoh Moses Amenhotep IV/ Akhenaten and his Lesser Wife Kiya. Therefore, she was sister to Pharaoh Tutankhamen!! Their children, including Aminadab, are included in the Old Testament of the Christian Bible! Cultures combining once more, to assist the Great Plan in its quest!?! Other than Mualeth, daughter of Enos and Noam, and Judah, son of Jacob and Leah, they all had centuries-long lifetimes.

It does not serve this writing to continue relating every generation. They are well documented for those who wish more details.

Step Four: The Change

Part One: King David and Queen Bathsheba

King David remains one of the most famous of the kings of the Old Testament of the Christian Bible. His exploits in war and at home are fodder for much folklore and legend. They are found amongst the writings and storytelling annuls of both holy and non-partisan people. The "Star of David" graces the flag of Israel even until today.

King David enjoyed many aspects of his monarchy, not the least of which was his absolute power. As children, we were regaled with stories such as David and Goliath, in which he was said to have bravely faced an enemy, Goliath the Giant, and slew him with only a slingshot as a weapon. *As it turns out it was not he, but an underling who did the deed.* The king was permitted to take the credit. The real hero, should he speak up, risked the very real danger of harsh repercussions. *Sometimes, so it seems, silence IS golden.*

The armies of King David waged war on many other nations and took as plunder the "spoils of war" including women. They were often the daughters of defeated rulers, such as Maacah, daughter of King Talmai of Geshur, China and his wife Tamar. He had many wives and concubines and many children. All told some twenty-one sons are documented amongst them. Not a single daughter is recorded. We know that there were obviously children of both genders in such a large group. In King David's time, women had already been limited in power and/ or control of their own bodies and their own lives. This is well evidenced by the number of women he took as the "spoils of war."

King David's closest friend and confidant was Uriah the Hittite, an astute soldier and a skilled leader himself. His name translated into English means, "God is My Light." He served as General and Commander of King David's vast armies. Under his capable command, many wars were waged and won. He was quite happily married to a beautiful woman named Bathsheba.

Once, when Uriah was away commanding the king's armies at war, David stood on the hillside above, watching the spring where the women bathed, *which was forbidden for any man to do.* He spied upon Bathsheba as she bathed and dried herself, and he was smitten. Even though she was already married to his best friend, he took her as his own. *Today we would call his actions rape!* When she became pregnant, he knew her husband had been away too long to hide the treachery. So, he sent word to the front that Uriah should come home for a break to spend time with his family. When the brave and loyal general refused, saying he could not desert his post, King David secretly ordered the soldiers to fall back from their leader in battle. Uriah was killed, *effectively murdered* by his friend.

Now, David was free to take Bathsheba as his wife. She had no choice but to comply. Their son died soon after he was born. Tongues wagged in private. The gossip was that King David's child was taken because he had been conceived in sin… a divine retribution. People were too frightened to say such things in public, where they might face harsh punishment.

Although their marriage began in a rather unpleasant way, Bathsheba (daughter of Eliam) persevered. Over the years, she bore David four sons named Nathan, Shobab, Shammua and Solomon. The House of David is easily followed through the centuries to many significant biblical characters including Joseph "the Carpenter" (descended from Solomon), Mother Mary (descended from Nathan) and therefore, Yeshua himself.

Even today, the exploits of this ancient and powerful king are legendary. His rather brutal and non-heart-centered ways of being, did much to alter the course of the Great Plan forever! <u>Unlike his ancestors, King David lived only 53 years</u>. The lifespans of his descendants shrank to what we now perceive as *"normal." This was a crucial turning point in the family annuls.*

Step Five: The Next Generations

We follow the story through Solomon, son of David and Bathsheba, and his wife Naamah Nabah of the Ammonites. King Solomon has been both revered and rebuked for his part in the annuls of history. One thing is for sure, his forty-year reign is a memorable one, any way you look at it! *Although not the oldest son of King David, he was favored as the heir to the throne, perhaps a concession to his mother, Bathsheba and her late husband Uriah.* He is well known for his work in building *Solomon's Temple*, a task he and his father had begun planning and amassing raw materials for, several years before David's death. (Ancient Jewish literature states that, because David had been a warrior king, with bloodshed on his hands, he could not build the temple himself.) It was a crowning glory of the united Jewish nation. The remains of the structural stones are still evidence of its existence today.

Solomon is also remembered as a wise ruler. One favorite story, is a tale of two women from the same household arriving at the palace, with one healthy baby boy. Each claimed that the other had rolled over in her sleep and smothered her own baby, and the surviving child was theirs. After some thought, King Solomon decreed that the baby should be cut into two pieces and shared equally by the two women. Of course, as he expected, the true mother quickly relinquished the child to the other woman, rather than see her baby harmed. So, the king knew the truth, and gave the baby to his rightful mother.

While watching a television show recently, which visited modern day Israel, and the ruins of Solomon's Temple, the narrator spoke of the following story of note. He stated that Solomon had talked of a visiting king from a far-away kingdom who had "appeared out of nowhere" to talk to him. He must have been from a kingdom "even farther away than the Land of Canaan" because he was dressed in unusual clothing and his features were very strange. His name was Melchizedek. He was very wise and talked of peace, kindness and other philosophical topics. Solomon was taken with this stranger, but never saw him again. **It is a matter of knowledge in many circles, that the Order of Melchizedek is a star-based Spiritual Order of high ranking. ** I mentioned this, when talking about Shem Melchizedek, son of Noah and Miriam.*

Continuing the story, another side of Solomon troubles biblical scholars to this day. We were taken aback by his father's many wives and concubines. There are seven hundred wives and three hundred concubines recorded for Solomon in the Old Testament! The scriptures set a limit to the wives a man could have at eighteen, beyond my understanding, as I write this. In any case, it seems Solomon did not think that rule applied to him!

During his reign over Israel, he amassed an unprecedented amount of wealth. The ten tribes of Israel were united, and it was a prosperous kingdom indeed. It has been referred to as the *"Golden Age of Israel "*. Many foreign rulers sought to build treaties and to create commerce with Israel. It was common at that time, to do so through marriages between the royal bloodlines. And so, many princesses and other women of note were offered to Solomon as wives. They brought with them, their own religions and deities.

King Solomon allowed some of his wives to continue worshipping their ancestral gods. He even accommodated this by building temples to a few of them. Rather than thinking that he was a kind husband to support his wives in the pursuit of their own religious practises, it was written into scripture, that he had fallen out of favor in heaven!

Solomon is blamed for the decline of Israel, and the division of the kingdom into Israel and Judea. And so, the saga of the Jewish people continued on toward the future, divided into smaller tribes each with their own rulers. The "nine lost tribes of Israel" scattered and Solomon's son Rehoboam ruled only Judea.

Step Six: The Egyptian Chronicles

This chapter is the perfect opportunity to expound upon the concept of soul groups. It has been known for a long time in spiritual circles, that souls tend to reincarnate in "soul groups." This means that, from lifetime to lifetime, we may share our journey, or at least a part of it, in the company of the same souls. We are not always in the same relationships each lifetime, once being father and daughter, once being siblings, once as spouses, and so on. In this fashion, we can assist each other to develop and grow, as we gain new perspectives in new roles.

This is not in any way to suggest, that only our soul group will share our life with us. On the contrary, many others drift in and out of our lives as we go along. It is also true, that we may reincarnate within the same family group, such as the same soul returning in the persona of a descendant of a previous manifestation. Over the years in this lifetime, I have encountered many such folks. As Mother Earth needs us to awaken to our "true spiritual self," so we remember!

Many of my biological ancestors have come from Egypt in different time periods. For a very long time, I have had inner knowledge of the Amarna period in ancient Egypt. I did not know initially what all those dreams, stories and memories were. I wasn't too concerned about it, as my world had always been filled with dreams and soul journeys.

There were visits with oddly familiar beings who lived under the earth, and seemed to breathe both water and air. There were ceremonies and initiations of mystical importance. There were my children, my family members and our lives. Much more was revealed to me through meditation, through visits to a Theravadin Buddhist monastery, where I became a frequent visitor for several years, and through my friendship and studies with a Hawaiian Kahuna. Revealing my soul identity further is not paramount to the tale, and may in fact, be an unnecessary distraction. You the reader may speculate, if it is important to you.

Moses Amenhotep IV (Akhenaten) was pharaoh of Egypt from 1571 B.C. to 1450 B.C. He has continued to be of great interest to so-called Egyptologists, to spiritual seekers and to the masses for a very long time. So, what about this man and his rule makes it so? He certainly was radical in his rule, in his beliefs, and in his appearance. Amenhotep IV created great changes in his time as pharaoh of Egypt. He angered the powers-that-be of his time, because he refused to wage war! For a very long time, Egypt had relied on wars to subjugate their neighbors, thus amassing the wealth and goods that fueled the kingdom's strength and power. Amenhotep IV did not want to continue this way of being. He moved the Egyptian capital to the new city of Amarna. He set aside the gods of past rulers in favor of the Aten, the Sun. This he said, was the true God of All Things. And he forbade war against other nations. The priests were not happy!

Pharaoh Amenhotep IV took the name Akhenaten to honor the Aten, as its true mouthpiece. His children carried the name of the Aten within theirs. His son Tutankhamen's name at birth, had in fact, been Tutankhaten, to honor the Aten or Sun God. It was later changed to protect him, as the ire of the priests and others grew against this new deity, and the peaceful ways of the new regime. As the crown prince and only son of Pharaoh Akhenaten, Tutankhamen did need to be kept safe.

Many stone carvings and paintings of Amenhotep IV and his family survive today, despite centuries of looting the sacred royal tombs and sites. They all depict an unusual looking man, with exaggerated features and an elongated skull. This has confused scholars over the ages. Some have thought he had hydrocephaly or some other birth defect. This type of anomaly almost certainly results in mental challenges and deficiencies. His keen intelligence and advanced skills in planning and ruling his kingdom does not bear out this theory.

Nefertiti Neferneferuaten, *"The Beautiful One"* as she is called, was the *"Chief Wife"* of Akhenaten, ruling at his side as queen and co-pharaoh. A less well- known translation of her name is *"The Pure One."* A famous and treasured bust of Queen Nefertiti survives as a tribute to her. Like her husband, she also exhibited the characteristic elongated head shape. For a very long time, popular myth held that she was portrayed that way, solely to mirror her husband's anomalies. In that way, it would somehow honor him and his unusual features.

Let's consider a different view of the situation. The unusual physical characteristics of this family, in relationship to others in Egypt then, or at any other time, may suggest they were from elsewhere. Another supporting point in this theory is that there are no recorded ancestral trails for Nefertiti, as there are for other ancient Egyptian royalty. *That fact alone is cause for curiosity, for the serious student of this well documented culture!*

Her recorded lifespan was a short one, from 1370 B.C. to 1339 B.C. During this time, she bore him six daughters. It seems she just *"showed up"* devoid of parents, siblings and/ or other family members. <u>Is it not possible, that she arrived as an adult from the Star Nations?</u> The title *"Pure One"* may imply her high vibratory level, in comparison to the humans already living there. As in other places and times upon Mother Earth, awakened ones (avatars) have come to assist our growth. Yeshua ben Youssef is one such avatar.

Princess Miriam Kiya Mery-Khiba Meryamon was also the wife of Amenhotep IV. She was called his *"Lesser Wife."* She lived from 1411 B.C. to 1363 B.C. She bore him two children. Her son Tutankhamen is the most widely known of the two. He is called "King Tut", "The Boy King" and other names. Most of us are familiar with his name and his story. His is one of a very small number of royal tombs of ancient Egypt, that had not been plundered for their treasures over the centuries.

The staggering wealth of treasure that accompanied him to the grave for his journey to the afterlife, was immense. His intricately crafted golden death mask alone is stunningly beautiful, awe inspiring and priceless. Only in the last century, Tutankhamen's tomb was opened to the sunlight for the first time in over 3000 years. When it was discovered, the world was in awe!!!

Tutankhamen had been married at a very young age, to his half sister Merytaten, daughter of Nefertiti and his father Akhenaten. By the time he reached the age of eighteen or nineteen, his wife was fifteen years old. The die was cast. It would not be long before Merytaten bore him a child, an heir. This would preserve the dynasty and secure its future for another generation. So, the disgruntled priests took the matter in hand, and the young pharaoh was murdered by a blow to the back of his head. Their treachery would be buried with him, until the discovery so many centuries later when the tomb was opened, and his mummy was found and studied. His name is known world-wide and comes to many minds immediately, when ancient Egypt is mentioned.

Kiya's second child, Kiya Tasherit, Tutankhamen's sister is much less well known. What is of great note about her, is her marriage to Old Testament prophet Ram Aram Israel, son of Hezron, 1589-1484 B.C. Many times, throughout the ages, Star Family members from different cultures have inter-married, to keep the Great Plan afloat. And such was this union. We see them in the biblical scriptures, as parents of Aminadab the prophet. (This was mentioned earlier).

*** This is only a small sampling of my ancestors in Egypt.
Others will emerge as the story continues. ***

Step Seven: Greece

Most of us grew up with tales of Mount Olympus in ancient Greece, and the mythical Gods and Goddesses who dwelled there. As a child, I heard of these *great beings*, who appeared, created Gaea (Mother Earth), the seas, the skies, the people, the animals and All That Is. They gave the people their teachings, and just as mysteriously, disappeared. I, and millions of others, assumed they were creations of mythical folklore, and not *"real people."* Imagine my surprise, when they showed up as ancestral relations in my genetic profile! I checked and rechecked, read, journaled and thought about it. As my research continued, I found links between the Olympians and the Old Testament prophets. Already, we have met some of them, such as Ham, Shem and Japheth, grandsons of Noah and Miriam.

They are connected to Alexander the Great, to the Egyptian Ptolemaic Dynasty and its pharaohs, and thus, to Mary Magdalene, and to the holy family of Christianity. The Roman Empire forever changed the fates and the roles of their descendants. Much more about these avatars will be revealed as the tale unfolds.

The "Holy Family" of Christianity

"The Awakened One" Arrives:

Judea in Jesus's Time….. an Overview

Firstly, it is certain that Yeshua (Jesus) was indeed, a real historical figure. He did live and walk on this Earth as an embodied man at the time that history has recorded. Many other things about him are, and have always been, hotly disputed. Before we can truly grasp the impact of this charismatic young man and the significance of his life, it is paramount to peak into the society within which he was born and raised.

For the last one hundred and fifty years or so, archeologists have been purposefully and painstakingly sifting through the sands of the Holy Land, to try to answer some of the controversy by finding scientific evidence regarding the man, the myth and the magic. There is an old saying amongst archeologists:

"The absence of evidence isn't evidence of absence."
…National Geographic, December 2017

When Yeshua was born, Judea and Palestine had been under the power and control of the Roman Empire for about sixty years. It was a rule fraught with severe sanctions, crushing taxes and cruel punishment for any resistance or non-compliance in any form! The occupying Roman soldiers wandered the kingdom at will, taking freely of anything they wanted… food, crops, tools, livestock, women…

The people were helpless to stop them and live to tell the tale. They were losing hope for a sustainable future for themselves and their children. Leprosy, tuberculosis, and other terrible diseases were rampant. Studies of graves in Roman-occupied Palestine at that time, by archeologist Byron McCane, showed that two-thirds to three quarters of them were occupied by children and adolescents under fifteen years of age. (National Geographic, December 2017) Conditions were similar all across Judea as well, under Rome's crushing dominion. In Yeshua's time, if you made it to fifteen years of age, you had a chance of living to experience adult life, marriage, children, etc. Not very good odds! No wonder people were praying for change!

Rome had no intention of slowing down their incessant quest to not only keep control of those areas already conquered, but to advance endlessly onward, until the Roman Empire encompassed *the entire world!* They were relentless, ruthless, shrewd, skilled military men. They did not know the word *"STOP."* Nor did they intend to! That is why they were able to conquer so many other countries and extend their empire into such a vast area.

The Jewish people were in jeopardy. Many kept their hopes alive with the ancient legends of a Saviour, a Messiah, being born to deliver them from bondage. And they prayed it would be very soon!

There was great interest in this Jewish prophecy, on the part of the Romans. They knew who was who in the Jewish world at all times. Careful records were kept on births, deaths and the hierarchies of Jewish royal families and their heirs. And, the Jewish Royal House was the House of David.

There is no doubt that Rome intended to rule the entire planet if they could! And there is also no doubt of the great and horrific persecutions they were capable of and willing to enact upon those who stood in their way. Nothing could be left to chance. They left no stone unturned. Cruel and tortured ends came to anyone who stood in their way, including many of Yeshua's family members. Deliberate twisting of truth occurred in order to gain access to power and control of the "Christianity" they manufactured.

Mother Mary/ a.k.a. The Virgin Mary

"Head of the Virgin" by Leonardo da Vinci… c. 1510-1513

Even today, after centuries of demonizing and degrading the status of women, Mother Mary has endured as a beloved saint, prayed to and worshipped around the world many times over, every day. Much controversy has arisen as to who she actually was, and how she got to be the mother of Jesus Christ. Was she a virgin, as we have all been taught for centuries? Was her son conceived through a magical interaction with an angel?

First, let's look at the word *"virgin."* To us, this means a woman or girl who has never had sexual intercourse with any man. There is no other possible meaning of the word *"virgin"* for most of us today. The first translation of the word by church officials was from the Latin word "virgo." This word actually when translated becomes simply *"a young woman."* Well, at eighteen years of age, she certainly was that. To be a virgin, as we understand it today, it would need to be *"virgo intacta."* Beyond that, to the Hebrew word in the older scripts, from which the Latin was originally translated. It was *"almah,"* a.k.a. *"a young woman" and held no sexual connotation at all.* The Hebrew word to mean a woman who had never united with a man sexually, would have been "bethula." *It was **not** the word used.* Whether a simple translation error or a deliberate alteration of fact, the results of this are monumental in our understanding of what really happened!

Mary's mother was Anna*** (see note below) and her father was called Heli Jacob. She was descended from the House of David through his son Nathan. Her husband Youssef/ Joseph was also descended directly from King David through his son Solomon! So, it is no small "accident of fate" that their first-born son Yeshua/ Jesus was a target of elimination/ murder by the Roman conquerors!

Mother Mary's lineage from King David (and therefore from Adam and Eve) is as follows: **David**, Nathan, Mattatha, Menna, Melea, Eliakim, Jonam, Joseph, Judah, Simeon, Levi, Matthat, Jorim, Eliezer, Joshua, Er, Elmadam, Cosam, Addi, Melci, Neri, Shealtiel, Zerubbabel, Rhesa, Joanan, Joda, Josech, Semeln, Mattathias, Maath, Naggal, Hesli, Nahum. Amos, Mattathias, Joseph, Jannai, Melchi, Levi, Matthat, Heli Jacob, **Mary**.

*** For a most interesting biography of Anna and her long life and times, please read Claire Heartsong's channelled book "Anna, Grandmother of Jesus." (Hay House Publishing) It will forever change how you may look at the story and mission of these remarkable people. ***

Joseph the Carpenter

Mother Mary's husband, Joseph (Youssef) ben Jacob was no ordinary carpenter or tradesman. As per his illustrious lineage, this is clearly true! He hailed from the Royal House of David. This made him a prince in his own right. The gospels tell us over and over, that Jesus was descended from King David *through his father's bloodline*. St. Paul, in his Epistle to the Hebrews states this as fact. Nowhere in the original texts is he named as a carpenter, woodworker or tradesman of any sort.

The book *"Bloodline of the Holy Grail"* by widely acclaimed biblical historian, Sir Laurence Gardner states that, the best translation from the original text was that Joseph was a *"Master of the Craft."* It really has nothing to do with carpentry at all! *It simply indicates that he was a masterly, learned and scholarly man!* That's it. Period.

It is widely written into scripture, that Yeshua was conceived by interaction between Mary and an angel, and not by the normal sexual relations between a man and his wife. One account that I found interesting is that Joseph was a 96-year-old man, assigned to "look after" her. That way, one could assume that they were celibate in their marriage. Still, that doesn't explain Yeshua's younger siblings, the other children in the marriage.

Actual records show that, at the time of their marriage, Joseph was 25 years old and Mary was 18 years old. That would be a normal marriage age for both people. As for s-e-x, it has also been a normal part of any marriage, at any time in history. It was never considered to be "evil" until **much** later when the church fathers said it was! How else could God's instructions to His children in Genesis to b*e fruitful and multiply* ever happen? Without sex, none of us would be here either. Admittedly, I was quite taken aback at the notion, that my own parents must have had s-e-x at least four times, in order to create my siblings and I…. having been raised in a very conservative home.

What is even more astounding to the "reality" we have all been schooled in, is the following! We have seen time and again, that when the Great Plan was in danger of collapse, the star beings have intermarried to strengthen their quest. And so, it was! Youssef's ancestor Judah, father of Peres, is also Jupiter/ Zeus of the Greek Titans. He is an ancestor of Mary of Bethany/ Mary Magdalene as well! If there was ever any doubt that she and Yeshua should wed and create children, that should assuage it once and for all!?!

Youssef ben Jacob, husband of Mary bint Heli, father of Yeshua ben Youssef's royal lineage from King David (and therefore from Adam and Eve) is as follows:
David, Solomon, Rehoboam, Abijam, Asa, Jehoshaphat, Johoram, Akhazia, Joash, Amaziah, Uzziah, Jotham, Ahaz, Hezekiah, Manasseh, Amon, Josiah, Jeholakim, Jeconiah, Shealtiel, Zerubbabel, Abiud, Elliakim, Azor, Sadoc, Achim, Ellud, Eleazar, Matthan, Jacob, **Youssef/ Joseph**

Jesus Alpheus ben Youssef/ Joseph...... The Early Years

The birth of Jesus (Yeshua) is very well documented in the Christian Bible. In many countries, children are raised on stories of the babe in the manger, the three wise men following the star and the shepherds visiting the "holy family" in the cold stable. This version of things is not actually, based on fact. Some of the variances put in place in this and other Bible stories by the Roman church, are not necessarily dangerous mis-tales at first glance. Jesus ben Joseph, was actually born in the Spring-time (not the usual Essene custom) by our calendar. He was more likely born in a house, which was customary practice in the area at the time. (Even today, there are very few inns around Bethlehem.) When strangers were in the area, such as Mary and Joseph, summoned there for the census, people took them into private homes. Although it was customary to lay an infant in a manger, we are talking about a clean, fresh wooden manger, in warm clean blankets, and not some dirty, hay-filled trough. And inside a home, not out in the stable with the animals.

The Roman church decided to alter many things in their version of the story. It was their idea to move the feast of his birth to December 25th, *near but not on* the Winter Solstice (Roman Saturnalia-Sun Festival) celebration. Therefore, any prospective converts would still get to celebrate at their usual time. As for the story of "the inns were full, so they wrapped him in swaddling clothes and laid him in a manger," I am not sure how it served the Roman church's agenda, unless to make him seem to be a poor commoner, and not an important royal prince.

The young Yeshua studied in the Essene school, which was quite separate from the regular Jewish education of the time. Their teachings were modelled on the star-based Essene dogma, rather than the existing Jewish lessons most children were taught. As a child, his teacher was Eucharia of the Essenes, who would later become his mother-in-law, when he married her daughter Mary Magdalene. His best friend was her son Lazarus. As boys, they played together much of the time. His childhood is largely unmentioned in Christian scriptural anecdotes.

"Head of Christ, Study for the Last Supper" … by Leonardo da Vinci c. 1495

Jesus's Personal Life & Ministry

So, what was so special about the ministry and teachings of the Christ!?! What made it stand out so vividly from the mainstream of its time? And every time? Let us remember firstly who he was. Yeshua was the crown prince of the Royal House of David, the rightful heir to the throne of Judea. Noteworthy of course.

In a kingdom without a king, ruled by a foreign power (Rome) he was no doubt, under their watchful eye. They became especially concerned when he began to preach, sharing his message with the people. Some turned away at his ideas, which flouted tradition. But many listened, believed, and followed him.

He talked about love. He sat on the hillsides amongst the sheep. He stood by the Sea of Galilee. He was humble. Women were not only welcomed, but were respected members of his "flock." Although the twelve biblical apostles we all know of were men, they were by no means the only ones close to him. Many women sat within his inner circle. Women like Martha, Mary the Mother, Myriam and Mary of Bethany (Magdalene).

And then, Rome's radar detected something they could not ignore. Yeshua married his beloved, as destiny demanded. His new wife, pregnant with their first child, was the daughter of Matthew Matteus, a wealthy and powerful Jewish rabbi (The Bishop of Capernaum) and a shamanic mother (Eucharia of the Essenes). Her maternal grandparents were an Egyptian Queen (Cleopatra VII) and a Roman emperor (Marcus Antonius) … Shakespeare's "Antony and Cleopatra." She too, was a shamanic princess. And so, the plot thickened. The more the people loved this new power couple, the less Rome did.

Although Yeshua's public ministry was underway, the Essenes stayed away from mainstream society as much as possible, as was their custom. They taught the Star Teachings of Caring, Sharing and Oneness to their children. They were peaceful and respectful.

Yeshua/ Jesus ben (son of) Youssef/ Joseph was entitled to the crown of Judea by blood. He was the next in line to lead his people. It was also apparent that he was a rising star in their eyes. Every day, more and more people flocked to hear him speak, beheld his healing "miracles" and declared their loyalty to him. He was fast becoming perceived as a threat to Roman authority and their dominance over a conquered and subjugated Judea.

Both Rome and the Essenes knew something must happen, something so big it would create great and lasting change! It's just that they were looking at it from opposite angles! One side, as the descendants of the original Star Council emissaries, saw the danger of the collapse of the now centuries old Great Plan. The other side, as conquerors of the realm of Judea, saw the danger of the oppressed Jewish nation rising from bondage to follow this charismatic new leader, this "Prince of Peace" to freedom from Roman rule. As we saw from looking at the earlier genealogy charts, both Mary Magdalene and Mother Mary were genetically tied to Roman ancestors. This somehow makes the whole story even more interesting to myself, and likely to many of you as well.

Here is where the Bible and reality deviate in the telling of the tale! **Jesus did not die at the crucifixion!** Again, **Jesus did not die at the crucifixion!** It is vital to grasp this Truth. It is true that he was brutalized, beaten, tormented and degraded. People are certainly capable of horrible acts! However, the direct mistreatment of fact, and distortion of story, have made such a mockery of the "Truth" that it is not Truth at all. The early church "fathers" (a.k.a. Roman conquerors) chose to distort the facts deliberately to their own ends.

As the beloved one hung on the cross, nails piercing his hands and feet, his head hung. He was thirsty and asked for a drink of water. So, the Bible tells us. The story goes on to say he was handed a cup of bitter vinegar, as a further sign of disrespect. What he was really given, was a Star Medicine which would slow down his heart-rate to feign death. In those times, there was no diagnostic equipment, such as in a modern hospital. Today, doctors might have detected the weak and infrequent heartbeat and respirations evident in such a state.

He was declared dead and could be taken down from the cross for family burial. As a safeguard, and for show, he was first subjected to a (superficial) spear wound. Scripture tells us the wound bled, which would not have happened if he was dead. Guards were ordered not to break his legs, as was usual in such cases. His maternal great uncle Joseph of Arimathea had previously paid a sum of money to Pontius Pilate, the Roman ruler of Judea, to remove the body and use his own prepaid tomb to bury Yeshua. So now, he was permitted take the battered body of his beloved great nephew down from the cross and carry him to the tomb.

The next part of the Plan needed to happen quickly! The 12 Shaman Priestesses of the star-based Order of Melchizedek entered the tomb through an underground tunnel. His mother Mary, and his wife Mary Magdalene, lovingly and tenderly washed his wounds and anointed his battered body. He was wrapped in fresh, clean cloth. As this was done, the Priestesses worked tirelessly. He had undergone much cruel and traumatic treatment during the crucifixion day. And so, his human body was very damaged. It was not an easy task, to heal his wounds and restore his strength. The healing process took the three days commonly mentioned in biblical and other accounts, as the time he was "dead."

It is neither a surprise that the first person he revealed himself to, upon emerging whole and strong on that infamous third day, was his wife, Mary Magdalene, the "disciple to the disciples." She was the *"Holy Grail"* the sacred vessel, and now more than three months pregnant with their first child, (my 50th great grandmother) Damaris (Tamar) Bint Yeshua. Tamar means "Palm Tree." She is often referred to as "Sarah" in surviving manuscripts, which has created some confusion over the centuries. The fact is, that "Sarah" refers to the title of "Princess." So, she would be Princess Tamar bint (daughter of) Yeshua.

It was the duty of every Messianic Bride, after the initial anointing of her groom on the wedding night with the precious spikenard oil, to carry the rest of the oil in a flask around her neck. She would not remove the oil flask unless or until her husband died. Then, it was her wifely duty, to anoint him again with the spikenard oil before burial. That was her intention when she went to the gravesite that morning. But of course, as we all know, he was not in the grave, but standing outside of it to greet her there upon her arrival.

It was never the wish or intention of Yeshua or other "holy ones" to be earthly kings or queens. Not in the sense that people created for them. True royalty rules within the hearts of every citizen of every land. It is not some duty thrust upon a select family, or hard-won in battle. For the crown lies heavy upon the brow. It propagates separation thinking, us and them, ruler and subject, rich and poor, and so on. These things are in direct opposition to the true teachings of Yeshua and his followers.

His mission was to restore balance to a planet that had long ago lost it. And he took it on willingly. It cost him dearly, as he knew it would. And yet, he still chose to speak freely, spreading the Essene/ Nazarene message of Love, of equality amongst all men and women. He was a pure being. He truly lived from his heart-center. His energy was uncorrupted. That is why people were drawn to him. That is why he could heal with his touch. _Had he lived long enough, his intention was to teach others how to do the same!_

So, who was this Jesus Christ, Yeshua ben Youssef anyway? He was not a Christian. Most of us can agree with this statement. Christianity was created after the crucifixion. He was not a Jew. This statement may be less plausible to many. After all, he was born in Judea, to the descendants of a long line of Jews, including the Royal House of David. In fact, he was the heir to the throne of Judea! But, not so fast! He was a Nazarene, an Essene, as were his ancestors.

Here, the story gets interesting. What the heck is a Nazarene or an Essene? _As it happens, they have long been recognized and known as ancient star-based spiritual groups._ Why aren't they in the Bible? Could it be, that the church "fathers" had a vested interest in obscuring evidence of Yeshua's true identity, origin and life, in creating and maintaining a largely fabricated version of facts? Were they willing to use unscrupulous, violent and murderous means to instill and propagate their lies? Yes! Roman military men were the conquerors and occupiers of Judea. They were not immune to the popularity of this charismatic young prince, or the crowds of adoring people who followed him, listening to him speak and swearing loyalty to him.

Nor, were they willing to give up their grasp on the lands and people of Judea! So, they seized the opportunity to "own" the Prince of Peace's story and recreate his reality to their best advantage! They re-wrote and/ or destroyed the documents created by the disciples and others close to him and denied the existence of the Shaman Priestesses like Mary of Bethany, to deepen and legitimize the patriarchal path they trod.

There is truth within the scriptures, although much has been deliberately removed, corroded, omitted and/ or mistranslated. A prime example of this is the tale of the love story of Yeshua ben Youssef and Maria Magdalena bint Matthew Matteus.

Mary Magdalene-The Messianic Queen

"The Magdalen" by Bernadino Luini… c.1525

Maria Magdalena of Bethany (a.k.a. Mary Magdalene) and Her Ancestors

One of the most controversial women in the Bible and arguably, in history/ herstory is Mary Magdalene. We have touched on this remarkable woman and a few of her ancestors and relationships already. Even after all of the time since she walked upon Mother Earth in that ancient lifetime, who, how and what she was is still unclear to many.

Was she a reformed prostitute, as the church fathers wrote into scripture some six hundred years after the Crucifixion? Was she a wealthy patron whose ample moneys helped Yeshua to forego employment as he wandered the hills and valleys of Galilee, sharing his teachings? Was she the woman from whom he drove out the seven demons? Was she his wife, and the mother of his children? One thing is for sure, she was an important part of his life and his ministry. He even called her *"the apostle to the apostles."* He told the others that they should go to her for advice when they didn't understand his words. *For she was the one who understood him the best.* So, what gives?

Let's start by looking at who she was, genetically speaking. We have read a bit about her ancestors earlier. They were important and influential folks!!

First, let's look at her paternal heritage. I have not been able to find records of her paternal ancestors dating back many generations, as is the case with her maternal lineage. Her father was Matthew Matteus Syro Levi Alphaeus, son of Jairus. Quite a title! He was a wealthy and influential rabbi in the Jewish faith, the High Priest of Capernaum. He was born in Galilee in 20 B.C. and died in Palestine in 40 A.D.

His father, High Priest Jairus of Palestine, her paternal grandfather, was also an important and influential figure in the Jewish faith. He was descended from the Pharisees and the Minoans. He was born in 60 B.C. and died in 60 A.D. in Palestine. Dan Brown's book "The Da Vinci Code" suggests that her paternal ancestry dates back to the kingly lines of Syria. She had two siblings, well known in biblical texts, a brother Lazarus, life-long friend of Yeshua, and a sister Martha. We will talk of them more later. The family home was in the town of Bethany.

Mary's mother was Eucharia Cleopatra of the Essenes, daughter of Marcus Antonius (Mark Antony) and Cleopatra VII Triphanae (Ptolemaic Dynasty). *Yes, **THE** "Antony and Cleopatra" of Shakespearean fame!* Cleopatra VII has been called *"the most powerful and wealthy woman who has ever lived."* As a matter of fact, the word "Cleopatra" denotes a woman of royal status in the ancient Egyptian world, a queen or ruler. And so, Mary Magdalene was not a pauper or without means. *She was a princess!* We have already looked at the fact that Eucharia was the teacher of young Yeshua, her son Lazarus (Yeshua's boyhood best friend) and her daughters, Martha and Mary (Magdalene).

The significance of her maternal grandparents and their part in the story merits its own discussion. Look for it later under the title Cleopatra VII Triphanae... Pharaoh/ Queen of Egypt

So, Mary Magdalene is descended from the Ptolemaic Dynasty in Egypt, through her maternal bloodline. This takes us back through all the pharaohs in this very long line of rulers. (Pharaoh Ptolemy I Soter, her many times great grandfather is called "the Saviour of

Egypt.") And to their queens (Cleopatras), often sisters chosen to rule beside their pharaoh brothers. And beyond that, to Macedonia (Greece).

Amyntos III (a.k.a. **Alexander the Great**), King of Macedonia (ancient Greece) was her many times great grandfather. He was the son of King Perdiccus Phillip II and a slave woman called Cleopatra of Macedonia, although his mother is often recorded as Queen Olympia of Macedonia, the king's wife. When he was a very young man of twenty years, his father was assassinated, leaving Amyntos III/ Alexander to rule Macedonia. He proved to be a skilled and capable general, brilliant and brave. He has been called by many, *"the greatest warrior of all times."* With a relatively small army of thirty-five thousand men, he pushed forward to vanquish many much larger armies. He swept through many nations, including Persia, Syria, the Phoenician Empire, Gaza, Egypt, Asia, Babylonia, Iran and onward into Afghanistan and India. What is astounding is that he did all of this in only eleven years! He was never, not even one time, defeated!

As he pulled back and began to organize his empire into a modern hub of eastern and western values and philosophies, he fell ill with a fever and died. By then, he had already established the ill-fated Ptolemaic Dynasty, from which Mary Magdalene later descended. This ties her to the Olympians of Greek history and gives her a very long-standing royal legacy! *Macedonia, Greece was the seat of the legendary Gods and Goddesses of Greek mythology. As it happens, they were real people, not just legends, and they were her ancestors..... and mine.*

I get it! I was skeptical when I saw them on my ancestry tree! What!!??! It all makes sense though when you look at it through different eyes. A very long time ago, when I was still (mostly) asleep, an elder told me that folks like me, from the Star People (Great Star Nations) Clan were/ are living in diverse cultures and locations around the earth. He said it was the Creator's plan...... It is not a stretch for those who have accepted the Divine Spiritual Perfection of Christianity's "Holy Family" to accept that others may also be Divinely Perfect. Is it?........ We had a peak into Mary Magdalene's Greek family members earlier in this book, as recorded in the Christian Bible's Old Testament. There they are, in many respected biblical accounts.

Following back through ages-old records, we arrive at the beginnings of Olympian Divinity. Mary Magdalene's many times great grandfather was the Greek God Cronos of the Titans, also called *"The Beginning of Life."* He is considered immortal. His wife/ partner is the Goddess Adrastea of the Titans, also called *"The Beginning of Life."* Much like Adam and Eve of biblical fame, they have long been considered the first to arrive on Mother Earth by many people. History and herstory may both speak to their truth. These beliefs are as valid as any others put forth over the many centuries.

They arrived on our planet some thirty-five hundred to four thousand years ago, and began their earthly stories. Because of the immense power of Rome, they have fallen largely into the category of "myth" rather than reality. However, they and the other primal deities of Mount Olympus, such as Gaea, Poseidon, Zeus, Jupiter, Nix and others, some of whom we have already encountered are as "real" as you and I. Like Yeshua's ancestors, Mary Magdalene's ancestors also arrived on this planet from the star nations as a part of the Great Plan.

Eucharia, Mary's mother was the daughter of an Egyptian queen. So, Egypt had a great significance for the Essenes. The *Right Eye of Horus Mystery School* is well known. It is synonymous with ancient Egyptian spiritual teachings. It is the school of the men's teachings and male shaman-priests. Much less talked about, is the *Left Eye of Horus Mystery School.*

This is the school of women, the teachings of the Divine Feminine and women shaman-priestesses. A very significant initiation for those who were ready, occurred in the Great Pyramid. I have read of it in writings by various authors and historians over the years.

The High Altering/ *the "Rites of the Holy Sepulcher"* was enacted in the so-called 'King's Chamber' of the Great Pyramid in Giza, Egypt. The name of this sacred chamber of initiation was based on the wrongful assumption that it must be a king's burial place. It was easily recognised as an important and sacred chamber. No consideration was given to a matriarchal, feminine oriented purpose for it. This all-too-common theme has belittled and obscured the true value of the contributions made by women over the many centuries of human existence on Mother Earth.

Continuing our story, it was necessary to undergo many years of preparations, initiations and ceremonies in order to be considered ready for this sacred rite of passage. Only the most highly evolved spiritual women were able to receive the *Rites of the Holy Sepulcher.* Here entered Mary of Bethany, Mary the Mother, Myriam of Tiana, and many other holy women, in their turn. As they lay entranced, guided and protected by the high priestesses, for four days and nights, their spirits journeyed to other realms. In this altered state, they convened with the Divine, learning and experiencing much. When it was time, the ministering shaman-priestesses assisted them to return to their bodies and reorient themselves to time and place. *Only those who were deemed to be at a very high state of Light and Understanding could withstand such an experience and return as a <u>Magdalene</u>. These were the Medicine Women of Yeshua's Inner Circle. And they were very sacred to he and the others.*

The "Holy Family" and their inner circle, were practitioners of the Essene ways of being. This included an understanding of the Divine as an inner, connected-with-everything Sacred Unity. *To restate, Yeshua and the star-based Essene group, did not see God as a male deity. And this Great Being lived within the human heart, not in some far-away kingdom. "Alaha" is the Essene word that Yeshua and the others used to describe "The Oneness" or "All That Is." Today's word "Allah", as used by Arabic speaking Christians, is derived from "Alaha."* An excellent source for much more information on this topic is Neil Douglas-Klotz's book "The Hidden Gospel." (Quest Books 1999)

And why were there so many *"Marys"* in the story? "Mary" at that time was not a name as we know it today. Rather, it was a title denoting "a faithful follower of the Way." So, Mother Mary, Mary Magdalene, and many other followers of Yeshua's teachings were called Mary...... Even today, Roman Catholic nuns, and most Roman Catholic girls, have been given Mary as a first or middle name.

Did Mary of Bethany marry? Yes. There is evidence that not only was Mary Magdalene a respectable woman, but she was in fact married to Yeshua ben Youssef (Jesus Christ). So, where is the evidence to prove the point? Firstly, it was well known until the Middle Ages, that Yeshua and Mary Magdalene were indeed husband and wife. Why would they hide the fact? It is the duty of every heir to the throne of every nation, to marry and have children. The bloodline must be continued!! It has been that way from the beginning, through all the generations.

How do we know she married? Where is it written? There are many unsanctioned or non-biblical scrolls and writings on the matter. According to well renowned biblical historian Sir Lawrence Gardner, "Mary is classified as the spouse and consort of the Messiah" in very early gospels that were "strategically excluded from the New Testament" by the Council of Carthage in 397 A.D. He goes on to state that "Cathar documents from Provence, as late as the

13th century, make it plain that in Gnostic circles, she was "always understood to be the wife of Jesus." As carefully as the editing and purging of anything resembling a Messianic marriage between Jesus and *anyone* by the Roman church, it is within the Bible itself that proof exists.

In the Essene tradition, the marriage takes place in two segments. The first is like a promise-to-wed or betrothal ceremony. They may be together as a couple for this beginning "trial period," but their union is not cemented together yet. This first ceremony is documented in the Bible, but not as the wedding at Cana, as most researchers have thought. It actually dates to the summer-time.

Rather it is another ritual gleaned from the Syrian royal traditions of Mary Magdalene's ancestors. Both Benedictine and Dominican records agree that her paternal ancestry ties her to the royal nobility of Syria. (Sir Lawrence Gardner) In the ritual of marriage, the Messianic bride anoints her husband with spikenard oil. This is a very expensive and precious oil from Damascus. It is **ONLY** used in the anointing of a Messianic groom by his bride. In the Bible, we are told of this anointing of Jesus by Mary Magdalene with sacred oil and using it to wipe his feet with her hair as well. They imply it is an act of humility and penance. But the fact remains, they did not omit the name of the sacred oil… *spikenard*. An oversight? Perhaps? After that event, she would carry a small flask of spikenard around her neck for the rest of her husband's life. She would anoint his body after his death, should he die first. It is no surprise then, that she would go to his tomb on the third day after the crucifixion with the sacred anointing on her mind.

The second is the formal marriage ceremony, and this took place in the town of Bethany, Mary's childhood home, only a fortnight or less before Jesus was crucified. We know that Mary Magdalene was three months pregnant then, for that was the custom in knowing when to complete the marriage. In that way, it was known that the union was to be a fruitful one, and the royal lineage would be continued, producing future heirs.

Their first child was a daughter, Damaris (Tamar) "Palm Tree" bint Yeshua. She was born Sept. 15, 33 AD, after the Crucifixion. We shall get to the real story of the crucifixion soon, which will explain how the young holy couple could bear children after that event! Then, in Essene tradition, four years later, she delivered a healthy son Josephus (Yeshua II). Another seven years would pass until she gave birth to Alain (The Grail King) in 44 A.D. This is the same year that the founding church "fathers" placed an edict upon her head, charging her with sedition. In modern terms, they hired hit men to murder not only Mary Magdalene, but her children and the other holy family members, *including his mother, Mary*. Inadvertently, they were instrumental in spreading the true word of Jesus Christ abroad, where it could flourish in the hands of his descendants, the Desposyni as they fled to Europe and beyond.

Mary was relegated by church dogma many centuries later, to the minor role of penitent prostitute to discredit her as the Messianic Queen she truly was. It does not add up, that the privileged daughter of wealthy, influential parents, pillars of the Jewish spiritual community, would ever work as a prostitute! This special child, educated in the Essene School, in the company of many biblical holy children, protected by doting parents, descended from royalty……. Illogical to say the least! In the teachings and tradition of Yeshua/ Jesus and others of the Nazarene and Essene groups, women were honored and respected equally with men. They were often powerful priestesses, teachers and leaders.

The first pope to publicly claim that she was indeed, a penitent prostitute, was Pope Gregory in 591 A.D., in his totally fabricated Homily 33. This is quite ironic in a time when, the Vatican prostitutes (courtesans) were numerous. They lived a life of luxury and were available to service popes and other high-ranking Vatican officials. In fact, the most well-known painting of Mary Magdalene as a prostitute was created with the pope's favorite prostitute as a model! By falsely portraying her as a repentant sinner, the pope and his cronies somehow felt absolved of their own sexual "misdeeds." At the same time, the lie made "truth" served to propagate the all male "Son of God" platform that church dogma demanded.

This Star Clan union was intended to restore the long-lost balance between the male and female members of humanity. This is a vital aspect of the Great Plan! _To be strong, healthy and forward moving, all members of a society must be equally important_. When the first star beings arrived upon Mother Earth, many thousands of years ago, this imbalance was already evidenced. Nor was it going to be easy to restore the natural order of things. As the reader is aware, it is still not restored today!

There is the knowledge that Mary and her husband Yeshua/ Jesus were equals! Each was a Master in their own right. During their lives together, they were inseparable. They shared everything, including their teachings and gifts. He loved her dearly and respected her status as a Shaman-Priestess. She was as much a sacred teacher as he was. In fact, she often was the teacher of the disciples and others. After the crucifixion, when the disciples could not grasp some of the complex esoteric dogma, Mary Magdalene helped them to understand.

It is the lies and betrayal of men who could not accept such power and status in a woman, that lessened her importance and disregarded her rightful place in the Christian annals. The destruction of many sacred texts with references by apostles and others to her Messianic marriage and children, her priestess status, and her integral part in Christ's ministry are unfortunate! _Women and girls all over Mother Earth, have paid a dear price ever since, as second-class citizens._

In 1896, a copy of the Gospel of Mary Magdalene was discovered in Akhmim, Egypt. As the finders were German, it was known as the Berlin Codex. To my knowledge, three copies have been found to date. No original has turned up, if it is still in existence. The Berlin Codex was never translated in all those years, until 1950. And, it would not be until 1969, under mounting public pressure, that the Vatican would openly acknowledge its Truths. Only then, the church finally admitted it had no proof of the "penitent prostitute" tale, and in fact that it was not true! They had known this for many centuries, but kept it quiet, as it served their "doctrine" too well. Its historical inaccuracy and outright falsehood were no secret to the church hierarchy. _It was they in actual fact, who had fostered it in the first place!_

All three known copies of her gospel have the same pages missing, seemingly ripped out long ago, by someone who didn't want people to read them. It is a passage where Yeshua is responding to a question about the way to be like he was, an awakened, fully realized human being (Anthropos). Apparently, the monks who preserved her manuscript for future generations, were not morally comfortable destroying the sacred manuscript as ordered by Rome, but at the same time, felt humanity wasn't ready to read and utilize his methods for Awakening on their own... a.k.a. independent of the church!

None-the-less, she remains one of the most commonly portrayed figures in art and sculpture. She was the most important figure in early Christianity, far more important than Peter or Paul. It is of utmost importance to clear her name and elevate her to her imperial place in Christendom and beyond. Only then, can we hope to restore the long-lost equality and balance to humanity and to Mother Earth!

Yeshua and Maria Magdalena
The Messiah and his Queen

What Really Happened?
Ancestral Memories Return-Maria Magdalena Speaks

"Why Master, why?" My desperate plea was directed toward my beloved, Yeshua ben Youssef. I called out through the crowds of people, who had come either to support him or to mock, jeer and torment him. He stopped briefly and looked directly at me before continuing his journey. **"Because, that is why I have come."** I knew that he could end all of this madness in an instant, by only wishing it so. And yet, he did not! His back was bleeding from the many scourges inflicted by a whipping he had endured at the hands of the Roman soldiers. He was wet with the sweat of his efforts in carrying the rough-cut wooden cross, upon which he was to be hung later that day. Even though he was a young man and in good health, he seemed tired.

He was swept away in the crowd, prodded forward by the points of the soldiers' spears. I, others in the family and followers of the Way, were overcome with anguish, fear and horror. Thinking of the children, I hurried to honor my duty to keep them safe and well protected from the public eye. Today of all days, it was very important!

The hours went on and on. Again, I found myself a part of the crowd who were witnessing this horrific event as it unfolded. By now it was afternoon. My beloved Yeshua was bent and stooped over. He was in great pain. People had peppered him with stones, fruits and vegetables, and/ or whatever they had at hand. Roman soldiers, tasked with marching him onward towards his execution, had further abused him as well. "Why Master, why?" He paused, as before and again, said gently: **"Because that is why I have come"** And the march continued relentlessly on.

Now, it was late afternoon, and his suffering was great! Upon his head was a crown fashioned from the thorny branches of a shrub, someone's cruel joke. Blood oozed out from the scratches and cuts it caused. People laughed cruelly and called him "King of the Jews." "Why Master why?" A third time, I implored him to end this madness. Again, he paused to look over at me with compassionate eyes. **"Because that is why I have come."** And the throng poked and prodded him onward. My hand went to rest gently upon my swelling belly, a most precious gift to our future world. And I wept with the others who loved him…….

Evening came. The plan to administer the bitter tasting Star Medicine when he asked for water while still on the cross had worked well. For, it had slowed down his breathing and heart-rate enough to have the authorities think he had passed away. (In the biblical accounts, it is recorded that he asked for water and was given vinegar to drink.) His Great Uncle Youssef ben Matthat (a.k.a. Joseph of Arimathea) quickly requested to take him down from the cross for family burial. As prearranged, Pontius Pilate ordered the soldiers not to break his legs, as usually done in these events, and instead allowed Youssef to take him down. _But please note, he was never dead!!_

We were now deep underground, in the tomb of his Great Uncle Joseph. They had lain the battered and bloodied body of my beloved husband Yeshua there. His mother Mary and I were tasked with bathing him, anointing him with the sacred oils, and wrapping him in clean cloth. We worked gently and tenderly, cleansing his many wounds. Tears streamed silently down our faces, leaving salty tracks in their wakes. All the while, the twelve Priestesses of the Temple of the Stars (Melchizedek) worked as quickly as possible. The severe brutality that he had undergone, at the hands of not only the soldiers, but others that day, had taken its toll.

The work of returning Yeshua to his full strength and vitality took the three-day period that is well documented in the Bible and elsewhere...

*** This memory came to me first, many years ago in a waking vision. I kept it to myself, as it felt somehow blasphemous or pompous to tell *anyone* such a thing. And as a practising pagan on a spiritual, non-religious path, it was all a bit embarrassing! It has returned since then many, many times and grown in depth and details. As I began to trust its validity, so too I began to understand the importance of sharing this and other sacred things that I have and do experience. They were largely confined to memory, and to journals and bits of paper stuffed in drawers, on computer shelves and in an old shoebox.

More recently, my mission to organise these anecdotes, to expand my knowledge and to research further, has come to bear heavily upon me. DNA analysis serves to verify quite a few family rumours, as well as my own dreams and visions... and much more. I began reading alternate sources, as well as the mainstream "accepted" versions of events. And so, slowly and steadily, this manuscript has taken form. Many others, as already stated, are also bringing newly recovered ancient information to the surface. A small sampling of their works, is listed in the "References and Related Reading" page at the end of this book. The seeker may find many other sources of information as well.

Never has herstory been more important to tell! History-only thinking has left out much of importance, twisting and distorting the "reality" of the human experience. The results are catastrophic for all of humanity and for Mother Earth!

Women hold the key to restoring balance! This has always been the case. In a world where men have long held the power and control, there has always been the fear that women would rise to claim our rightful place as warrior, equal in every way to our male counterparts! This is that time! It must be! Elders and seers of every culture have foreseen this for a very long time. **We are the ones we have been waiting for.** We are the maidens, the mothers, the crones! We are the seers, the mavens, the wise women!

For the last six thousand six hundred and twenty-five years, we have been experiencing the Time of the 5th Sun, which has proved to be a time of discord and chaos upon Mother Earth. Just very recently, we are ushering in the Time of the 6th Sun. This is the time of a return to balance, a time of restoring the Divine Feminine to an equal place beside the brothers who are at the helm of the earth-ship. The qualities of creation, nurturing, caring, sharing, death and rebirth lie within this realm. And it is present in men and women. The wheel has turned. The Magdalenes awaken.

Time has come to enter the Temple of the Rose!

The Holy Grail

"The Magdalen" … by Bernardino Luini… c. 1525

The *Holy Grail* and what exactly it is, has been hotly debated throughout the ages. Knights, kings and commoners alike, have sought to find it and to claim it as their own. Speculation as to what it is, where it is, and exactly what magical powers it may contain are the subject of many stories and legends. King Arthur and the Knights of the Round Table are a prime example of the fascination around the Holy Grail, which exists and persists to this day. As with many other things, incongruent with the teachings of the *"Prince of Peace"*, violence and bloodshed have followed in the wake of the endless quest to find this ancient relic.

One common idea is, that this mythical item is the actual cup used by Yeshua at the Last Supper. Another is that Joseph of Arimathea, Mother Mary's uncle collected Yeshua's blood in this sacred vessel at the crucifixion. Both remain as popular theories. Neither is verifiable.

Others, myself included, have quite a different idea. The Bible, after many edits, alterations and re-translations has omitted all mention of the notion that Yeshua/ Jesus Christ was married. However, had he not been married, the duty of all young men in Judaic tradition, and especially more so, as the crown prince of Judea, it would most probably have created a much more note-worthy stir! There is quite a body of evidence to suggest, that not only were they married, but they had children together, including Damaris (Tamar), Yeshua II and Alain, the Grail King.

As previously mentioned, Mary of Bethany (Magdalene) was a wealthy young woman in her own right, daughter of a high-ranking Jewish priest, Matthew Matteus Syro, Rabbi of Capernaum. Her mother, Eucharia Cleopatra of the star-based Essenes, was a Cleopatra, an Egyptian princess! To even suggest that their daughter would need to go into prostitution to survive is non-sense.

The Holy Grail is not a physical relic like a cup. It is the genetic code of the Christ, surviving through his union with Mary Magdalene. She is the "Holy Vessel" mentioned in the scriptures.

Rome did not want to allow this truth to surface. If Yeshua had descendants, then they, and not Rome would be in control of the legacy left by Yeshua and his family. As the rightful heir to the throne of David, Yeshua was a clear and present threat to Rome. The people increasingly and adoringly followed him about the countryside listening to his speeches. Many declared him the long-awaited Messiah. They began to find hope and promise of a better future in this young man. And now, with a powerful, newly pregnant wife by his side, he might very well overthrow the Roman dynasty and *"set the people free"* just as in the prophecies of old.

So, the decision was made that Rome must decree and carry out the execution of this prince in short order, before he could do any greater harm in usurping their authority. Pieces fell into place in rapid succession. He was brought before the High Priest Caiaphas and charged with a rather thinly constructed crime, found guilty, and sentenced to crucifixion, the most popular method of death used by Rome at that time. It was usually carried out in full public view, to discourage others from any thoughts of unlawful behaviour. And so, it was.

Part Four: The Aftermath

In CE70, only a few short years after the crucifixion, the Imperial Edict ordered that all members of the House of David, be arrested and eliminated until no one of royal stock remained. Of course, this would include all Desposyni, all descendants of Yeshua and Mary Magdalene. It would also encompass those who were descended from his brothers and anyone else who were close relatives of the "holy family." In this way, Rome didn't risk an uprising by the Jewish nation they had conquered and ruled for so long.

By then, Mother Mary, her daughter-in-law Mary Magdalene, and others of the House of David, had been safely taken to Britain by Arch Druid King Bran Fendigund, husband of Anna Enygeus, the Prophetess. She was the daughter of Yeshua's brother James the Just and Anna, a daughter of Mary Magdalene's brother Lazarus and his wife Salome. Another melding of star ancestral family lines at a time of great chaos on the Earth and in the Great Plan!?!

Saint Judah Kyriakos was the last Jewish Bishop of Jerusalem. He was, according to Epiphanius of Salamis, a great-grandson of Yeshua's brother St. Jude. According to Malachi Martin in his book, "The Decline and Fall of the Roman Church," there was a meeting between Pope Sylvester I and the Jewish Christian leaders in 318 CE. Desposyni had always been governors of the Jewish Christian church, as legitimate blood relatives of Yeshua's own family. A Desposynos church leader should be named once again. They asked that the Sabbath be restored, as well as the Holy Day Feasts and the New Moons of the Bible. Also, that Jerusalem be restored as the mother church, and donations be sent there. Pope Sylvester sent them away with the admonishment that, from now on Rome was in charge of Christianity, and they must accept the fact and go home. They were told that the salvation of the people no longer rested with Jesus and/ or his heirs, but "God Himself" had bestowed that right upon Emperor Constantine. As far as we know, this was the last meeting between the two groups. And from here on, Rome ruled the church as they did the Roman Empire…. With an iron fist and without mercy on dissenters.

Cleopatra VII Triphanae... Pharaoh/ Queen of Egypt

Cleopatra VII, last pharaoh in the ill-fated Ptolemaic dynasty of Egypt, is well remembered in history. **She is in fact, the last pharaoh of Egypt! Ever!** Although not commonly known, she and her consort Marcus Antonius are the maternal grandparents of Mary Magdalene, as previously mentioned in this writing .... She merits her own pages in this book, as we will soon see. She has been touted by many, as **the most powerful and wealthy woman who has ever lived.** Pharaoh/ Queen Cleopatra VII ruled at a time when Rome was taking over the world stage and holding everything in their tight-fisted grasp. Her true and accurate life story is still somewhat shrouded in mystery, more than two thousand years after her death. Nor has her burial place and/ or her earthly remains ever been found and verified.

She is the "Cleopatra" in William Shakespeare's epic play "Antony and Cleopatra." She has been variously portrayed as a temptress, as a sexually indiscrete, promiscuous party girl, as a shrewd leader and as a scholar of note.

First, we will look at the Ptolemaic Dynasty, which ruled Egypt from 332 B.C. to 30 B.C. The thing is, they were not Egyptian at all, but Macedonian (Greek). Over time, they spoke both Greek and the Egyptian dialect(s) of their time as rulers. When Alexander the Great (Amyntos III) of Macedonia conquered Egypt, he wanted to create a line of rulers, which was comprised *exclusively* of his own family members. And so, he established the Ptolemaic Dynasty and set them up in the new Egyptian capital of Alexandria. In order to safeguard the bloodline, this often meant brother/ sister marriages. The male rulers were the pharaohs and their sister-wives the cleopatras that ruled by their sides.

It appears that, there was much duplicity as the Ptolemies lived their lives. They jostled for power and control of the wealthy Egyptian Empire. Sometimes, this meant an untimely end to the lives of one or another pharaoh or cleopatra. And so, life as a Ptolemy was not without its risks. Even as children, family members had their own entourage of protectors, advisors, administrators and alliance builders.

To the last generation, there were no marriages outside the family and/ or multiple marriages. In accordance with Alexander's instructions, given long ago, the incestuous, all-in-the-family marriages were continued. (There may have been unrecorded dalliances with others here and there.) It had previously been the norm in Egypt, for the pharaohs to have harems, with many women in them, in order to secure a number of potential heirs. Alexander/ Amyntos III himself, had been the child of King Perdiccus Phillip II and a slave woman, Cleopatra of Macedonia, although his mother is often recorded as the king's wife Queen Olympias.

Moving forward… Cleopatra VII was the daughter of Pharaoh Ptolemy XII. She grew up in the palaces of Egypt. She was an astute scholar, learning to speak nine languages fluently. She studied philosophy, politics, history and mathematics. She was consumed with learning, as evidenced by her creation of the Library of Alexandria later in her reign.

As she reached adulthood, she lived in the shadow of unrest inherent in the chaotic and unsettled times. Rome was growing ever stronger and posed an increasing threat to Egypt. When her father died, his will named she and her brother Ptolemy XIII as co-regents of Egypt. She had to be smart and act decisively, in order to survive, thrive and protect her nation. A plot by her brother to wrestle control by force ended badly, with his demise. Now Cleopatra was in control, and would rule for some two decades. Her official co-regent was her younger brother Ptolemy XIV. He posed no threat for the time being.

By now, she knew she needed the support and protection of Rome to stay in power. In effect, her very life was likely at stake otherwise. And so, she had herself (famously) smuggled into Julius Caesar's quarters and seduced the much older Roman ruler. A move that would serve her well. She produced a son by this relationship, and named him by the lofty title, Ptolemy Caesar Theos Philopator Philometor (The God Who Loves His Father and Mother). Greek speakers called him Caesarion, "Little Caesar." *He is the only recorded son of Julius Caesar!* Things were in good order for now.

The considerable coffers of Egypt were available for use in financing the political and military expenses necessary in Rome's ever-expanding quest for world dominion. A symbiotic system that worked well for both countries for a time. Caesar had a golden statue of his lover installed in the Temple of Venus the Mother. This established her as the Mother Goddess to the Roman people. It gave validity to their union, and officially recognised Caesarion as his son.

Caesar was becoming more and more dictatorial and in 44 B.C. it became his undoing. He was murdered by his fellow senators. Cleopatra fled home to Egypt with Caesarion, then three years old. She had to act quickly. Her brother/ co-regent died by poisoning, leaving her as sole ruler. She elevated her young son Caesarion to the title of co-regent. It was known that he was Julius Caesar's son, and her hope was that he would be her successor after her death.

She knew she still needed a powerful Roman protector. Roman Triumvir, Marcus Antonius was already interested, having met her some years earlier. Their relationship is infamously recorded, and largely embellished by Hollywood and other sources. William Shakespeare's play "Antony and Cleopatra" has been fodder for many schools' class studies for a very long time. Movies abound, most famously Elizabeth Taylor and Richard Burton in the title roles. She is seen as a temptress, rather than the deeply complex character she really was.

This relationship proved to be a longstanding, fruitful and successful match. They produced several children, notably a set of twins named Cleopatra Selene (Moon) and Alexander Helios, and Eucharia, who would later become the mother of Mary Magdalene. As previously with Julius Caesar, her riches gave Rome security and his protection gave she and her countrymen safety.

However, Octavian (later Augustus Caesar) a nephew of Julius Caesar, wanted to rule Rome. His forces overtook those of Antony, first in 31 B.C. in Actium, and then in Alexandria. The game was up! Rather than wait to be killed by Octavian, Marcus Antonius took his own life by sword. It is believed that Cleopatra VII also took her own life, rather than become the spoils of war. She had an extensive knowledge of poisons and their uses, so may have poisoned herself. The fanciful snake bite by asp is not accurate. This much we do know. In any case, it has made a very romanticized story of the events surrounding the deaths of this powerful pair!

Antony and Cleopatra VII had come so very close to absolute power. There is also great speculation of murder rather than suicide. We may never really know for sure! But, one thing is certain! Had they lived and retained power, the world we live in might be a very different place today!

Desposyni... The Next Generations

It does not serve this writing to elaborate on all of the succeeding generations in the family archives. Many modern writers and researchers have been and are revealing carefully hidden, deliberately disguised Truths. They are easily accessed by anyone who wishes to do so. These revelations are reweaving the patterns in the colorful tapestry of humankind. As much as the reader may not equate some of the next players with Desposynic and/ or mystical roots, I imagine neither did many of them, in their lifetimes.

In my next book in this series, I plan on elaborating on successive Desposynic generations and how they have and do affect our lives even today! Many surprising folks grace the birth charts and death records in the very long line of Desposynic ancestors. They lived in many nations and social classes, from rags to riches and back again. Some of those still living today, are as influential and well known as those long ago!

For the moment, we will leave it at that, and carry on with this book's pages.

****

(Faces of God, Goddess, Creator, Allah, Jehovah, Yahweh, The One, The Universe)

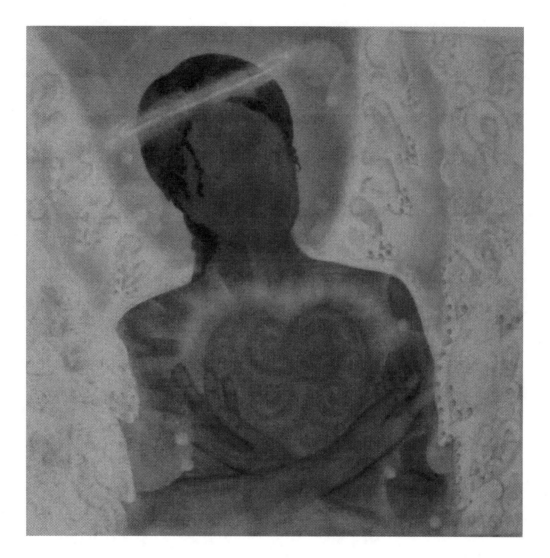

God is an all-encompassing being
which holds everything within its light.
And yet somehow, each of us looks into its reflection
and sees a different face mirrored back at us.

What if we ourselves are that Great Being!?!

"Our job is to love others, without stopping to inquire whether or not they are worthy." This quote from Thomas Merton speaks to the universality of humankind. *Everyone is worthy of love.* In as much as we are unique, we are all the same. Literally, as well as figuratively. As part of *The Whole (God)* we are part of each other.

If you are still reading this book, you have figured out that I am a poet. I include here, a small sampling of poetry I have written over a span of many years. Some, has come from my own adventures and events, a glimpse of my heart, a splash of the colors that paint my life journey. Some, has come to me spontaneously during meditation and/ or while doing my morning journal pages. And, there are tales of brothers and sisters I have met/ walked with here and there. They convey the common emotions, struggles and events that shape us individually and collectively into T*he Whole*. Anyone else's story is also yours and mine. Therefore, I have not chosen to specify which of them have come from my personal experiences, from those of folks I have encountered and/ or which of them are more ethereally derived.

At first glance, it may seem odd or even counterproductive to include poetry and prose about fears, insecurities, pain and unwellness, as well as all the cool stuff about love, peacefulness, growth and spirituality. Here's why. These *"challenging"* events and emotions are often the life lesson teachers we have come here to meet.

Having compassion and understanding for the folks in these pages, not only *assists their* healing and growth, but yours and ours, as *The Whole*. May you resonate well with something herein. Perhaps, you may even catch a glimpse of yourself here and there.

Time Wasted

fear eats away

at the quiet places

until there is only

that familiar anxiousness left

that un-nameable thing

that grips you

by the innermost

crevices of your soul

immobilizing isolating numbing

stealing your present moments

and replacing them with

a deep abiding regret

at music ignored

and songs unsung

and poems unwritten

guilt sets in
at so much time wasted

Who Am I?

"pretender" "faker" "wanna be"

wtf! is that me!?!

am i less or am i more?

what are all these questions for?

the sky is full of endless sparks

the sea is full of endless sharks

circle in its endless spin

as it turns, it draws me in

i try my best to look away

to keep the faith another day

to love the life that i am choosing

to let go of the fear of losing

might as well abandon fear

play the game well while i'm here

for if i keep on playing small

i'll never play the game at all

either way

one day

i will say

"can't stay"

<u>Cocoon</u>

being raw and openly exposed to the world

allowing the stares and (sometimes) glares of others

to conjure up a cold and biting wind which whips at your body

threatening to carve a cruel path of destruction in its wake

can wreak havoc on your self determination

and undermine your hard-won freedom

all of the limits instilled in you by others

while you were still just a very small child

corroded your innocence, your self-love and your magic

and settled quietly without apology into your very core

making most of your decisions for you

until this present moment

and even now it is a somewhat uneasy task

to stand your ground and resist the fear of judgement

that gently urges you to return in an instant

to the safety and solace of the cocoon

where no one can see your vulnerability

or think you unworthy

thankfully it is much too late for this type of setback

you are you and you are awake to All That Is

you hold your head high and smile at life's challenges

you know they are only opportunities to grow

you stand in your light and breath deep breaths

you can do this, you are doing this

What If...

the same scenario repeats itself

over and over, faster and faster

in never-ending loops…

the monkey mind descends

into madness

and what if ensues

what if it had gone another way?

what if…

what if…

consumed with alternative endings

that somehow absolve the guilt and shame

as if the very conjuring

would make it so

putting right the wrongs

rendering a blameless peace

and a spotless return to innocence

sometimes too much can be revealed

like the time you were taking a drawing class

and the live model thought he should be completely naked

so he dropped his towel

Unplugged

sometimes

in the quiet hours

when all the world sleeps

and dreams a dreamless dream

the wine weaves a peaceful pattern

a soft synthetic samadhi

a convenient collapse

sometimes

barriers lifted

i melt into nothingness

sometimes

in the quiet hours

when all the world sleeps

i choose to become liquid

flowing into the void

i am nothing

i am everything

i am free

sometimes

Tattoo

rainbow colors splashed

in living color

across living canvas

telling tales of magic and miracles

long hidden away

this is me

i am that… I AM

clear pictures still raw

from the artist's needle

brave wounds exposing

the innermost journey

laid bare to the world

no way to hide it now

no room to wonder what they think

will they recoil… revile… reject

it matters no more

for at last

in taking risk

i am free

Fly

glimpses of the past

cannot be kept too long

just learn the lessons, heal the pain

let go, and then move on

resist the urge to tarry

or hold on to the rhyme

the songs we've sung, so long ago

are moments trapped in time

looking to the future

wings spread open to the sky

i find the strength, to face the wind

not walking, now i fly!

*"Out of suffering
have emerged the strongest souls,
the most massive characters
are seared with scars."
...Kahil Gabran*

So, does this mean our highest purpose here in these human disguises, is to suffer!?! No. Not really anyhow. It means, that to learn and grow, it is important to experience life deeply, to find the parameters set out for us, and to go beyond them. Often, this may separate us from the so-called "norms" in our lives. As we stretch our wings in other directions, we may become ostracized from the pack. As social creatures, it is an uncomfortable feeling to not fit in, to not belong. And so, suffering ensues!

Wounds (suffering) will appear, then reopen and bleed again and again, until they are cleansed and dry long enough to heal. This process (often) involves acknowledgment of those wounds and how they got there. What keeps them there? What to let go of and what to keep in order to heal? How to move forward without those oh-so-familiar wounds?

And yet, upon closer inspection, as painful as these (metaphorical) wounds might appear, they are actually our greatest life lessons. They will heal, sometimes quickly, sometimes less so, as we learn why they were there in the first place, and absorb their insights. *Of course, it is a planet of free will. So, in essence, we don't really need to do anything at all!*

In the Indigenous (1st Nations) cultures, none are more revered than the "white hairs," those who have lived long enough to have their hair turn white, like the snows of winter. For, it is assumed that during their long lifetime, they have accumulated Wisdom. Valuable Wisdom, that can help their communities to stay strong and thrive. So, folks wear their white hair with pride! We can learn a lot from this!

I remember many years ago, my paternal grandfather, at the age of eighty-four years young, saying the following to me. "Child, the day a person gets up and goes about their whole day, just to look in the mirror before bed and say honestly; 'today I have learned nothing,' then it is time for them to go. Their lifetime is finished."

He is a wise and gentle spirit. He lived a long life and raised many children. He taught them all to honor and respect themselves, each other, Mother Earth and All That Is. He worked hard and shared what he could with those in need. His marriage to my grandmother lasted some 60 years until his passing. His legacy lives on in a myriad of descendants.

The Flower Lady

she grew many kinds of flowers

in her tiny garden plot

she always had kind words to say

and time to spend

when you wandered by

she knew all of us by name

she remembered our stories

asked after our grandchildren

bought treats for our dogs

and shared the prettiest blooms

we took her gifts for granted

the flower lady was always there

so we felt a great empty space inside

the day she wasn't waiting

to brighten our morning

Never-Ending Journey

she was a gentle soul

soft around the edges

sane in her insanity

paddling backwards

in a sea of sharks

always surviving

somehow

fresh wounds festered

amongst the scars

screaming silent testimony

to the madness

that was

her life

yet there was no stopping

she continued on in her way

as you do when

you see no other options

Peter's Story

daylight brings familiar craving

sees his life as not worth saving

moves from where he spent the night

shuffles off to face the light

morning crowd of passers by

never look him in the eye

never stop to lend a hand

never try to understand

rolling up a dirty sleeve

crack cocaine a brief reprieve

crumpled down in pouring rain

with trembling hands he finds the vein

and once again he drifts away

another time a brighter day

long ago a happy life

a home a child a loving wife

but father son and holy ghost

desert him when he needs them most

return him back to cold and pain

and craving to get high again

Shasta's Story

going to the food bank

was a turning point for her

shattering the illusion of 'all right'

but you do what you need to

when there is nothing left

to feed your kids

cupboards laid bare and ravaged

in an attempt to fill little bellies

"i am trying my best, but there is no work!"

words of despair spoken

to no one in particular

sharp shards of guilt and shame

jutting jagged testimony to

events that shattered her world

cutting gaping wounds

in the carefully scripted

reality she clung to

tearing loose the safety nets

ripping away the veil of illusion

leaving her bleeding raw open

and oddly relieved alive grateful

"if this is the worst of 'not all right'

then i am stronger than i thought

and i am ready to dance with

whatever comes my way"

The Princess and the Pauper

gazing out the palace gates

the princess spied a child

her dress was torn, her feet were bare

her hair was long and wild

"come in and play and be my friend"

said the princess with a smile

"it's quite okay if you can stay

at least a little while"

the pauper bowed and curtseyed

and sadly, turned away

"my liege" said she, "the die is cast

i can't go in to play

it's not for us to change the rules

oh princess, don't you see?

the ways that we shall live our lives

are bound by destiny"

the little princess thought a bit

"you're just the same as me"

-two little girls from different worlds-

"two friends are all i see!"

and so it was, the girl came in

torn dress, wild hair, bare feet

the princess said, "bring cheese and bread

my friend and i shall eat"

Even one small act of kindness by a little child, forever changes the Energy of the Whole!

A Sudden Departure... Mourning the Grandmother's Passing

dark mysterious goddess

dwelling now on distant shores

far beyond space and time

carefully woven fibres unraveled

with piercing precision

in a flash of destiny

never to be undone

rites of passage celebrated

sacred ceremony of honor

lays the body to rest

spirits gathered

under full moon sky

bring comfort to

the sisters left behind

numbness subsides

and chaos envelops the beloved ones

until blessed acceptance

soothes the wounded hearts

and lifts the veil of illusion

that separates us

long enough to say goodbye

and find the grace

to let her go

Crone Song

i am spirit in human form

woven into the sacred circle

my hair, as soft as silk

pales in the autumn days

to a muted tone

and silver threads appear

the moon's pull remains strong

but she no longer exacts

her quota of monthly flows

what is remains and grows strong

i am a crone!

my voice sings out

to join the millions of others

who through the ages

have stood here…

the sisters and the mothers

wise-blood

woman of mystery

teller of tales

sewer of seeds

aged and ageless

A Slow Going Away

"i love you" he says softly

holding the hand that holds his heart

gazing at the familiar face of the woman

he's loved for almost fifty years

and he still sees the same beautiful young maiden

he wed one summer day long ago

she returns his gaze

with a look that says "who are you?"

she wonders why this elderly stranger

has rivers of teardrops silently staining his cheeks

and why is he here anyway?

doesn't he have a family somewhere

awaiting his return

only rarely now moments of lucidity appear

amongst the clouds of confusion

when the remembering returns

it brings the gentle touch of true love

real and alive and wonderful

the promise of joyful sunbursts

glittering glimpses of long ago

sustain him in his lonely vigil

in the moments and the hours

when she is still so near and yet

gone so far away from him

Dawn

morning light falls upon the earth

and catches hints of gold

upon white wing feathers

the angel still stands strong

babe stirs in his sleep

she remains as if transfixed

hesitant to disturb this moment

wishing it could last forever

knowing all too soon

this peace shall vanish in time

and her babe shall be torn away

into a sea of madness

propelled by destiny

into the world again

into the hurt and pain

and for the first time

she is afraid

Angel

when the Angel left

a gaping hole remained

an empty space so vast

it sucked the very life from me

and in its wake

i wondered if i would survive

the loss

even remotely intact

"Angel come back!"

yet she is gone

and (somehow)

i am still here

we are still here

this is the way it has been

for eternity

i am tired

In the End

in the end

as the dust settles

signalling the finish of this lifetime's struggles

comes a deep abiding peacefulness born of wisdom gained

while journeying upon the face of Mother Earth

one tiny step following another

each step a sequence

in destiny's path

it is always

the letting go of darkness

and the return to light that allows

the true nature of the traveller to shine forth

revealing the soul's perfection at last laid bare

to shine forth freely forever

as the dust settles

in the end

★Tools of Transformation★

<u>Now What!?! Where Do We Go from Here!?!</u>

"If you are depressed
You are living in the past.
If you are anxious
You are living in the future.
If you are at peace
You are living in the present."
...Lao Tzu

"The secret of change is to focus all of
your energy, not on fighting the old
but on building the new." .....Socrates

What I Know:

"Don't die with your music still in you." ... Dr. Wayne W. Dyer

In a long-ago meditation, I asked for some directions on how to go forward in good ways. I pondered the ages old questions of 'Why am I here; Where/ who is our Creator (God/Goddess); Is there a Creator (God/ Goddess) or just us; What should I be doing with my life', etc. This is what came to me. And this is how the Spirit Speaker introduced herself, word for word.

"You have all the tools. Open the toolbox."
...Spider Woman, Weaver of Webs, Dawn Star, Keeper of the Rainbow from the Dog Star, Sirius

When we come here as a tiny new-born baby, we remember why we are here. Earlier in this book, we looked at this beginning place in our lifetime(s) when everything is laid out, like some magical map before us. And then, like a cloak of forgetful slumber, our spirit self settles into its human disguise and adopts the illusions of the *"real world."* The human experience is largely affected by our family of origin and the cultural, religious, educational, financial, health and other boundaries, that allow us to *"fit in."*

It is somewhat like a dog who is used to being tied on a certain length of chain. Even if allowed more freedom, s/he will invariably be more at ease within the *"normal"* range. Oh sure, they may explore a bit farther afield, and even try to see just how far they can get to on this longer tether, but will mostly, just plop down in the usual place, content that it is their spot.

In moments of clarity, we feel awesome and open to the possibility of shining forth our inner light. Often though, we get bogged down in our mundane, earthly tasks and pursuits. We are afraid to open ourselves to maximizing our true potential, and just "go for it." The current times strongly urge us that changes need to occur **NOW**, not in some distant era! *Everyone* __now here__ *cannot be* __nowhere__*!*

As much as we are all one Great Spirit Being experiencing itself as endless sparks of energy, we are also disguised as "individuals." So, let's explore these two aspects of the divine, that we are comprised of (duality), and how this affects our experience as human beings.

Firstly, it must be said, that we do each and all, no matter who we are, where we come from, and what belief system we have adapted to, experience "reality" in our own ways to some degree. This is our ego self, our mind, thinking its thoughts, filtered through our "individual" lenses, as stated above.

"Thoughts become things... choose the good ones." Mike Dooley (www.tut.com) coined this phrase a few years ago, in the era of Rhonda Byrne's book/ movie "The Secret." I have also heard the late Dr. Wayne W. Dyer express this same idea in his talks. He used to say; "When you change the way you look at things, the things you look at change." Many years ago, a wise Anishinaabe elder, whom I love as a brother, used to tell this story to illustrate the point. I have never forgotten it.

One day, a wild thunderstorm was raging. Three men sat together on the front porch of a cabin, whittling their sticks and chatting. They were well protected from the wind and rain. The first man said; "Oh, I am so terrified! What if the lightening hits the cabin, burns it down, and we are all killed!?!" The second man said; "Well, Mother Earth can sure use the rain. It's been so very dry this summer." The third man said; "Awesome! Powerful! Magnificent! A'Ho! The Thunderbirds are cleansing Mother Earth and restoring Her to Purity and Peacefulness!"

It's all in how you look at it. And the good news is, it's up to you! If your current situation is less than peaceful, reframe your thinking around it. No matter how dire the circumstances you find yourself in, *you've got this!* Remember the tv show "Fear Factor" where people were made to face their most terrifying fears!?! All fears OUTSIDE themselves! Big challenges for all of the contestants! Some did a better job of it than others. All were changed by the experience!

In the elder's story, we may all see bits of ourselves in each of the three men, at different times, and in different circumstances. Most of us travel back and forth amongst them. The trick is to look INSIDE, to dwell in our heart-space. *There is no fear there, only love.* In the heart-space, we are all the third man!

The other part of the human persona seeks to belong to a group. We have looked at this aspect of ourselves throughout the book. It is hard to walk wise and to be free of "group think." And yet, it is entirely possible. Each of us is a perfect spark of the Creator/ God/ Goddess/ Allah… the One, and at the same time, housed in human form. Our current (temporary) human persona is also host to its own version of "truth" and "reality." Both may change many times in each lifetime. And so, duality exists within everyone.

What if no one on this planet took the risk to be different? Then nothing would happen. We'd all be stuck. "Nothing ventured, nothing gained." An old adage, but just as true as ever. It is not acceptable in a world that strives for even the smallest level of enlightenment to preserve the status quo, at the expense of anyone or anything that shares Mother Earth with us! Or of Mother Earth Herself for that matter!

So, take a chance. Venture forth. Be your awesome self, freely and fully! So, what if you get hurt? So, what if you feel foolish? Stupid? Wrong? Different? The point is, you did something you believed in! Great job!

So now, ask yourself:
1/ Where am I now?
2/ Where do I want to be?
3/ What is *one thing* I can do *today*, to get closer to my goal?

And pause right now, for a few moments, to really ponder the answers…. Write them down, if you feel like it. Keep it simple and short. Use everyday language that makes sense to you. Never mind lofty, trendy concepts that tend to go "over your head and under your feet." Be patient with yourself. You are well on your way there, whether you can see it or not! If you're unhappy with your life, make changes. Even small ones add up. Take relentless baby steps forward in the direction you seek.

Decide on a desired outcome, for yourself and on a broader scale as well. *Picture yourself in that end place (goal)*. **FEEL** how it feels. Taste it, Smell it. Wear it…… touch it! **BE IT!** Wow! Amazing! Excellent! Awesome! Fabulous! Whoo Hoo! As you focus on it, clarity sharpens. **YES!**

Now, let it go!… Let the Universe/ God/ Goddess/ Creator put the pieces in order. Follow your gut as your footsteps flow forward. Allow things to unfold. Resist the urge to insist on HOW you will get there!

What!?!… No way!!!!

Detachment:

Some weeks ago, I was out for my morning walk with my dog, enjoying the (socially distanced) air, along the beautiful walking trails in our small city. This is always a highlight in my day. Now, as you will know by now, I am a poet at heart. So, not surprising that when I speak to Spirit (*my Heart-Space*) seeking answers, they may come in poetic form. These words sprang forward to me. I was "asked" to repeat them over and over, until I got home, then to write them down. The wording is unlike anything I myself would *"normally"* create, so they seem even more significant to me.

Here they are, as they came to me that Spring-time morning.

> *"detachment from the outcome*
> *is not an easy task,*
> *like tryin' to drink a dram of ale*
> *from out an empty flask"*

So, what is that about then!?! Aren't we supposed to picture the outcome? Yes, we are, in general terms, to create a knowing of where we want to walk towards…. But not at the expense of the present. If fixated on the future, we may miss out on the present moments we are being granted. Why do you think they call this moment the *"present?"* Because it is a *gift* for us…. Right!?! Every moment experienced, up until this exact moment, has led each of us to this one!! Every moment, whether we might see it as *"good"* or *"bad"* ….. Trust the process and never mind the "cursed hows" (Mike Dooley… www.tut.com) as to the manifesting part. Do your best and leave the rest. There is no accident or cosmic joke at play, that has us here, living through these unprecedented times. Nope! None!

So, surely decide _where_ you want to be. Decide _why_ you want to be there. Decide _what_ your life may look like. Take those relentless baby steps in the *general direction* of where you want to be. Let Spirit decide _how_ to get you there. All is well! As Mike Dooley says in his book *Manifesting Change*: "The most important 'things' anyone can put in their mental imagery are not the physical details but the emotional ones." In short, **FEEL from the end (goal) as if you are already there**. Spirit will then work overtime to create that end place (goal) and get you there. A Hawaiian Kahuna whom I was fortunate to meet and study with, used to also share this wisdom. He would say; *"Think from the end." "Feel your goal as if it is completed." "Act as if you are already there."*

WAIT! What Am I Thinking!?! Me!?! Moving forward with grace and ease!?! Of course, the answer to this question is a resounding *"YES!"* *A moment only becomes a movement when you move!* Get it!?! It's all those little baby steps forward we talked about earlier. This is what gets the One/ Spirit in gear, setting the stage you need to get to your goal….

"Rest if you must. That is okay. But, do not tarry too long, child. Move forward on your journey. There is not as much time as you think". These words came to me (longer ago than I might wish to re-member), in meditation. They are from a Star Spirit Guide, Spider Woman, whom we met earlier.

Another favorite quote I always like to share with students and friends, is from Henry Ford, the founder of the wildly successful Ford Motor Company. He was a visionary, a man who had a dream of where he wanted to be (a goal), and took those relentless baby steps until it was made manifest. Mr. Ford would say: *"Even if you're on the right track, you'll get run over if you just sit there."* He got it! And look where it led him to.

Gratitude:

"Gratitude makes sense of our past,
brings peace for today,
and creates a vision for tomorrow."

... Melody Beattie

In any quest for enlightenment, peace or a positive direction in our path, gratitude is a perfect place to embark from! Well, what do I have to be grateful for? I'm not rich, beautiful, well-known, living in my dream world, etc....... Many folks do not see they have much at all to be grateful for! To them, I say the following:

Did you get up this morning? Are you breathing? *Great job!* That is a good place to start. Most of us have a lot more to be grateful for too! Yes, we do! "I feel grateful for my home, the food I eat, my family, the big tree in the yard, walks in Nature, my good health, my dog, my job." Whatever comes to mind, say *"thank you." Feel grateful!* When we are in the *feeling of gratitude*, many more things to be grateful for are drawn to us! It is the *emotion* or *feeling* that creates the energetic field to match. And voila, things begin to manifest in our lives that match the *"gratitude vibe"* we are putting out. Like attracts like. Thoughts become things. Take a few moments every day, to focus upon what is *already in your life* to be grateful for. Notice new things begin to appear that you feel gratitude around. Set goals. Think big! Why not!?!

I am reminded once again, of the movie several years ago, by Rhonda Byrne and friends, "The Secret." A woman with cancer appeared in the movie. She repeated the words, *"Thank you for my healing"* over and over every day, *with a feeling of great gratitude,* for several months. Thinking from the end...... And guess what? To the astonishment of her doctors, her cancer disappeared! She was cured of a terminal disease, because she had *gratitude* in her heart, because she *felt* the healing as if it was already complete. The One (God/ Goddess/ Spirit/ Creator) took care of the how, and moved into place the pieces to make it happen! Whoo Hoo!

Now, the proverbial "they" say it takes twenty-one days to change a pattern. *I have belonged to a "21 Days of Gratitude" group for about two years now....* Is it because we suck at gratitude? No. It is because we are finding that, the more we focus on gratitude, *no matter what our outer circumstances at the time,* the happier we feel. So, we just keep doing it! It's a Win-Win!

Sometimes, we find gifts in the challenges we may face here and there in our lives. Clarity often comes, in recognizing ourselves in those around us. I have often had a big *"Ah Ha Moment"*, as the struggles of another resounded within my own heart! None-the-more-so, than with loved ones, family and friends. It is hard to not become entangled in a web of enmeshed energies. Remember the word *"detachment"* from earlier? Well, here it is again!

In releasing the *"ties that bind"* a.k.a. psychic cords/ attachments we may have between us, we set ourselves and others free. They have been lovingly created and maintained in the mis-taken belief we are *"helping"* or *"rescuing"* our child, grandchild, spouse, friend, and so on.... Because we love them. Right!?! We don't want them to be hurt, sad, lonely, or in any other negative state. Right!?! Stop it! *It's simply not our job!* In actuality, we do not (consciously) know what their end game is, what lessons they are (cosmically) here to learn, what their bigger picture is! So, trying to mess with that is inappropriate.

*** Please note, that I am in no way implying we should not support our loved ones, or intervene if they are in physical danger. That is a given! In releasing the energetic "cords," we in no way reject them, or stop the love between us! ***

We love them unconditionally, support them emotionally, honor their triumphs, and comfort them when they struggle. We may often experience many human incarnations with them in different personas and relationships to help each other learn and grow (soul groups).

An elder once told me, that we are being gifted these human journeys, to experience human things we cannot possibly experience in the world of spirit. Our current human disguise is temporary. Our spirit self is eternal.

The Fixer… a.k.a. The Band-Aid Lady/ Gentleman

Many of us on the healing path are band-aid people. We want to "fix" everyone and everything in the misguided notion that they are "broken" or "wounded." Of course, we feel we are the _only_ ones who can do it! And we somehow know how it is all supposed to be! Dr. Phil might call us "Right Fighters." But we do not see ourselves that way. We are nice kindly folks, just trying to save others from suffering. Right!?!

Wrong! In a 3D world, dogmatic rights and wrongs, rules and regulations have been set solidly in place for millennia. They never worked. They still don't work! And anyway, it all depends on which dogma (indoctrination) you are schooled in. It really doesn't serve you or your "fixee" to stick to any restrictive, narrowly focused way of being.

As Dr. Bruce Lipton says, we are like a computer, which is running a certain program someone placed there long ago, when we were a very small child, under the age of seven or so. We absorbed it like a sponge. Now as adults, unbeknownst to our conscious mind, this program runs away, on remote control most of the time. It is not our true self. It is just old programming. As we expand our awareness and raise our vibratory rate, we begin to awaken to the magnificence we truly are. And we figure out how to over-ride the program and experience brand new and exciting things! Whoo Hoo!

It does a great disservice to try to expunge the data in anyone else's data bank. Nor, to try to "fix" them. _They are not broken!_ The challenges we and others face are the very teachers we have come here to meet. I am just beginning to understand my life on higher levels. This is a time of great change on Mother Earth. And, as we have already discussed, this is a planet of free will. So, I honor and respect others as they navigate their life paths. As a reformed band-aid lady, it is beyond hard, to watch others, especially beloved family and friends struggling, hurting, in pain.

"No pain, no gain" … an old saying that persists. Is it nonsensical? Perhaps. Why not uplift others from their suffering!?! Why not share with those in need!?! I am in no way, advocating ignoring suffering if/ when I may be able to share food or other necessities of life with others! Or a loving hug, a listening ear, a caring heart! We are all one great Sacred Circle, each a part of the other. Every life matters!! Caring and compassion are never amiss!

What I am talking about here is the desire to take over someone's autonomy with (usually) unwanted advice, or to salve their wounds in the assumption that you are "helping" them somehow. And you may well be. But, all those band-aids don't let the air at the wounds, and may impede the healing process. Sometimes, better to just let them know you love them. Listen if they wish to share. Give advice only as asked and without judgement. Keep your band-aids in your pocket. Allow them to sort out their stuff as they go. Let them know you are proud of them no matter what!

Judgement

Having been on this planet as long as I have, and remembering a few other visits (incarnations) here, there are a few truths I have learned. One of the most important is one of the most difficult. Brendon Burchard sums it up well as follows: *"Judge less. Be happier."* When navigating the ins and outs of this tenuous and at times fragile existence we call life, it is very easy to get caught up in the persona of a *"Right Fighter"* (Dr. Phil). Right Fighters assume that if they are "right," then everyone else who has a different world view/ opinion is therefore "wrong." So, they cast judgement upon everyone and everything. In an instant, lines of separation are drawn. Everyone and everything are slotted into their places. And so, it goes. As Brendon Burchard so aptly pointed out, when we judge others as wrong, we are not as happy. The negative emotions wreak havoc on our positive ones, rendering us into a negative state. The very assumption that we are following the only <u>right</u> path and that all other paths are <u>wrong</u>, is itself <u>wrong</u>. It is inherently flawed!

"Judge not, lest ye be judged"
……..Yeshua/ Jesus Christ (The Awakened One)

And yet we do. I do. You do. It is a distinct human foible, to judge. Always has been. We make ourselves and those like us right, normal, good. We make everyone else wrong, deviant, deficient in some way. We highlight perceived differences and declare them "flaws." We imagine these flaws exist in everyone who is not philosophically, culturally, racially and politically just like us. We point accusing fingers at the rich, the poor, the less educated, the more educated, the powerful, the powerless. We believe our personal path is the true voice of the divine. We draw strength and self value from feeling superior. And so, we are bigots! Pretty hard facts for anyone, who perceives themselves as spiritually grown-up enough to accept the concepts of the human family, the oneness of all, live and let live, and such-like.

Like the reader, I have and do struggle with all of this as well. Being of the Desposyni (descendants of the Christ) does not excuse myself or any of the multitudes of Desposyni currently living today, from such challenges. In fact, it never has, over all the ensuing centuries. Of course, like most others, I would like to say I have risen above such things. I cannot say so. Like all of humanity, consciously or unconsciously recognized, it remains a dream and a goal.

What exactly is judgement? The Merriam-Webster Dictionary defines it as such: "the process of forming an opinion or evaluation by discerning and comparing," "a proposition stating something believed or asserted," and/ or "a formal utterance of an authoritative opinion." As synonyms, it puts forth the following…. "belief, conviction, feeling, opinion, verdict, view." It appears that it is neither an exact science nor all abiding. As many other earthly tools to handle life, it is only that… a tool. It is subjective, arbitrary and, as the dictionary points out, a "feeling", "opinion", or "view." *In other words, an illusion, a trick of the mind.*

On this planet, there are many concepts that fall into the category of judgements we make. Some are very widely held. Recently, the term "Fake News" was coined by former US president, Donald Trump. While many folks are not too fond of the terminology, it is a fitting and apt way to describe not only the current political scene, but the validity of the judgements we make every day about every subject we encounter. They are Fake News! No matter how they began to nest in our mind, they are the subjective meanderings of others, carefully groomed, managed and nurtured until they took up residence there. They can be uprooted, altered, or even discarded. But often not without great effort on our part!

How does someone recognize a judgement for what it is? Fake News! We each and all have so many things inside us, ideas, opinions, prejudices. Some have been there so long, that they have become automatic responses to input generated by the outside world. We carry them nestled safely away in the unconscious mind. We may not even be aware they are there, unless or until something or someone triggers them. And there it is: **judgement**!

"Oh my, where did that nasty thought come from? I had no idea I felt like that! That's horrible! OMG! I am a bigot!" (aghast) "Well, after all, they were wrong to act, dress, pray or whatever the way they do. It's not right! It's not normal! It's different than me!" And so, the justification of one's position begins. A little voice somewhere in there tells you that your "feeling," "opinion," or "view" may not in fact be valid, or exclusively correct (remember Merriam-Webster Dictionary) …… Momentarily you falter, pausing for a moment or two. Sometimes, you listen and even acknowledge your flawed thought processes. You may promise yourself to do better. You may work to change your narrow-minded thinking. Mostly, you just push reason aside and carry on as before. You get the picture….

Mistakes:

So, what is a "mistake?" Does everyone make them? Are they bad? Are they a flaw in a person's character? Does God get mad at us if/ when we make mistakes? Or, are they actually divinely guided life experiences? Should we try to "fix" everything we figure is a "mistake?" ... or just let it lie, allowing the pieces to fall where they may? Is there one right answer, hiding in the heavenly ethers somewhere, just out of reach? Or are there as many answers as there are people, events and circumstances? Food for thought. *Soul Food ... Food for the Soul.*

Let's start with the following definition of the word "mistake" from the popular and respected Merriam-Webster Dictionary. These statements about the word "mistake" reflect upon the true meaning of the word. As a verb, it is defined as "to misunderstand the meaning of or intent of... to misrepresent" and/ or "to blunder in the choice of." As a noun, "mistake" is "a wrong action, statement or judgement proceeding from inadequate knowledge of, misunderstanding of, or inattention to someone or something."

None of this implies a deliberate deception, fueled by malintent! **This is VERY IMPORTANT**! To be harsh with self or others regarding a mistake made is to negate the very nature of the word!! Rather to understand and sum it up as follows; "**I did the very best I could at EVERY given moment, in conjunction with the level of understanding, the tools and the resources at my disposal at that time.**" For this, my friends, is a much more accurate description of what a mistake really is! Mis-take 101. Follow with Re-take 102... if and when appropriate.

Sometimes, we realize we have made a mis-take right away... like when we try to take a certain picture with our camera, and miss. I have heard the term miss-take for the resulting image. So, what then? Of course, if anyone, including yourself has been placed in any impending danger by your mis-take, right action is imperative immediately! That is obvious! No matter the circumstance, any embarrassment or inconvenience you might face, pales in the face of the safety of anyone involved in the matter. End of! So, a quick assessment of the situation and its circle of influence will let you know if immediate action is warranted.

If not, ***STOP***! Do not react. Wait until the dust settles and you can think for a moment or two! Feel the fallout in your heart-space. Then, you can ask your higher self (God-Self) what is the best way to proceed. Above all, <u>act</u> rather than <u>re-act</u>. *What would be the higher purpose in trying to "fix" your mistake?* How would it affect you? How would it affect others? Sit with this query for a bit, even overnight, or for a few days, until your answer comes. <u>**Please**</u>.

It is (likely) safe to say, each and all of us have acted too quickly, out of a sense of trying to be honest, trying to fix things, trying to be congruent with our beliefs and truths. This is usually so **WE** will feel better, **not** the person we are making amends to, in our quest to make things right! And sometimes, in some situations, that band-aid does help to calm us down, at least in the short-term. Eventually, we forget about it, or at least relegate it to the back burner, and move forward to newer issues and events...... and so it goes.

What if, just for a moment, we decide to turn the whole mistake conundrum on its head? Is it possible or even likely, that there are gifts in our errors/ mistakes? Stopping to absorb the impact, and to put it into perspective, we can learn from each mis-step, wrong word or uninformed choice. This very writing has been spawned by such a thing. And, not without a great deal of self-restraint on my part either! *I SO WANTED to fix it asap!*

I was attempting to express the great degree of love, respect, honor and positive regard I had for a very special member of my Soul Family, who was about to move to a far away country, So, I spent a lot of time in trying to get the words just right! It was important to me to create just the perfect words to convey how I felt. As I wrote and rewrote the pages, after nearly two days of working and worrying, I felt that it was time to put it away, no more editing, no more checking and rechecking for perfection! A certain uneasy feeling suggested that something was hiding therein, something "wrong", and it was to become an important teacher. It would be revealed later. And so, I dutifully put it away. The next day, it was given to the intended recipient to read later in private, so we wouldn't dissolve into emotional tears in front of everyone.

Imagine my horror later on, when I salved my curiosity and reread the manuscript copy. There it was!! I discovered a rather unfortunate grammatical error/mis-take in the very heart of the document!?! Twice!?! Zounds!?! What should I do? My reactionary part wanted to own up to it immediately, grovel, and rewrite/ reprint the pages with the proper corrections made. It was all I could do, not to react accordingly!

Then, I remembered my admonishment from the ethers. So, I stopped. I asked myself if those two little grammatical mistakes would negate all the loving thoughts I had placed into the writing. Of course, the answer was "no." Would it be a wise and right course of action, to draw attention to them at the expense of the intention in the written words, thus changing my friend's focus every time she read the pages? Again, "no." So, I just sat with it and breathed.

So glad I did. She is an intelligent woman, and no doubt saw the "mistakes." But when she contacted me to thank me regarding the letter, and other things I had prepared for her, there was no mention of grammar. We talked long and shared warm gratitude for our Life Journey time together, mutual respect, loving-kindness and heart-centred kinship. Beyond the human based mistakes, that could have colored our last few in person interactions, lies something so much more intrinsic and important, the heart and soul's expression! God/ Goddess/ Creator/ Allah/ All That Is!

I now consider this little circumstance a gift, a gift for me, a gift for others who may come across this page. I intend to expand myself when mistakes occur, as they will sometimes. I intend to look for the gift(s). I intend to see beyond the event, beyond my reactions, to another place of learning and understanding. Sometimes, hasty actions that seek only to make me feel better are short-sighted and may stop the growth of the Whole.

Are there times when consciously admitting to and owning your mistakes, and making amends is appropriate? Of course, there are! Someone once said that the hardest words ever spoken in any language are these: *"I am sorry!"* Wisdom spoken here for sure! If you have been hurtful to any other being (mis-taken), and it is safe, prudent and appropriate to do so, do it! Every situation and event is unique onto itself, as unique as you/ we are. And as similar….

…..A great Rule of Thumb in ANY situation is the following…..
Given the choice to be right, or to be kind, always choose kind!

I am responsible for my ideas, my words, my mistakes, my opinions, my beliefs, my actions, and the consequences of my actions.

I am not responsible for the ideas, words, mistakes, opinions, beliefs and/ or the actions of others. Nor am I responsible for the reactions of others to my ideas, my words, my mistakes, my actions, and the consequences of my actions.

Please read the last two statements again… and again… This is paramount to acceptance of self, to creating and maintaining self-worth, and to walking in step with God/ Goddess/Creator/ Allah/All That Is (a.k.a. Your Heart-Space)!

Poor Self-Image is one of the major contributing factors that keep us stuck in the *Loop of the Lost*. In today's fast paced, unbalanced world, the treadmill is spinning out of control. We might feel so disempowered, it seems easier to just spin, to go along for the ride, and hope for the best. Fingers crossed for a soft landing, if it all crashes to a stop some day!

No, you say, that is not me! I am spiritual! I meditate. I pray every day. I go to church/ synagogue/ mosque/ sweat-lodge/ circle. I love animals. I recycle. I donate to charity. I pick up garbage when I'm out. I got this! Excellent! Great job! But, are there deeper layers lurking just below the surface? Perhaps!?!

Even the most evolved beings, when in human form, may falter in the knowing of their own Divine Perfection. There have always been avatars, seers, shaman and sages incarnate upon Mother Earth. This we know, no matter the country, culture, religion or spiritual path we have learned and adopted in our lifetime here. They have walked in every corner of the Earth, for millennia, sharing their gentle heart-centred wisdom freely with those who crossed their paths. As you, the reader of these words, I too, have, and do, examine those secret layers, hidden away in the deepest recesses of my being. I meditate. I pray. I ask the ancestors, the angels, the spirits and the guides. Sometimes, the hardest thing is to just get out of my own way, and "allow."

Allow the answers to surface. Accept those truths as they surface. Know my divinity!! Even after all the centuries of tarnish, **I AM LIGHT!** Easy to say. Easy to write those words. *Not as easy to fully BE LIGHT.* At least, not in the human mind self. So, if I cannot accept my own LIGHT, how will it affect me on a personal level? How will I know to keep moving forward on my path? Let's look at a few examples that have let me know……

Recently, I was honored to be a part of a small circle of powerful Medicine Women. Of course, I accepted their invitation right away. Still, a small voice somewhere inside wondered why I was chosen!?! Would/ could I carry my part!?! They did not know my heritage as Desposynos, not really anyway, not at that point. We were all spiritual women, and most of us have known each other for some time. Of course, I was made welcome, I was respected, and the ceremonies were powerful! A day to remember for all of us! Each of us was representative of one of the four directions. Our prayers and intentions were of a healing nature for Mother Earth and all who dwell upon Her face, and for All of Creation. It was magical. We all felt the magic deeply and profoundly.

The most profound gift I received on a more personal level, was the gift of insight into my own worries about inadequacy, about not being a part of, i.e. *Low Self-Esteem.* During the event, at a certain small segment, I experienced a feeling of exclusion, of being separate from, of imperfection… the details are not important to this writing. The concepts are. What had been, unknown to my human self, a great attempt at honoring me, on the part of the other women, was *mistaken* by me as exclusion. It was not the intent. It was my own *mis-take*…

Remember Merriam-Webster Dictionary… "misunderstanding someone or something, based on inadequate knowledge of the situation, thus making a faulty judgement" … and it was generated by me! It was a very valuable and lasting life lesson for me. Always come from a place of an open and compassionate heart and a goodly (godly) intention, and you are supported fully on all levels. I AM a perfect part of the Creator of All Things. <u>As I AM enough, so i am enough!</u> Will I make other mis-takes here and there? Most likely. I am in human form. I pray to recognize them quickly and re-frame my thinking.

Low Self-Esteem is anything that precludes recognizing the Truth about ourselves. We are already perfect. There is nothing we need to have, be or do to enhance that state! Nothing. Not a book, or a workshop, or a video, or a ceremony, or an attunement. Nothing. No thing. We are already loving, loveable and lovely!!! In many religious and spiritual paths, we are taught that, we are made in the image of God. If this is true, then how can we possibly be imperfect? Is God not perfect? Well then…….

Forgiveness!

Forgiveness is not only necessary in order to move forward on one's path towards manifesting Divine Oneness, it is paramount! This is not to say that it is, or ever was, easy. It is hard. It is a task that takes great strength! It may not (typically) be accomplished by one quick stroke of the proverbial pen! And, it IS worth the effort! Holding resentment, anger and pain within one's being, lowers the vibratory rate/ energy level and makes it much harder to move forward. In essence, it creates and maintains self-generated chains and prisons within one's heart.

Depending on the magnitude of events that have caused the animosity/ anger/ hurt, it may be more or less difficult to forgive. And yet whenever, wherever, however the hurt occurred, the past is just that, the past. Everything you have experienced to date, has brought you to this exact moment. *Now! You are in charge of now!* "You can't reach for anything new if your hands are still full of yesterday's junk." (Louise Smith) So, the only person who is suffering now from past hurts to self, to family, to anyone or anything, is you!

Some time back, I was in a very uncomfortable state of overwhelm, related to what seemed to be devastating life circumstances on a few fronts. At the same time, I was doing beading classes in the company of a small inner circle of women I love, my heart tribe if you will. I had considered not attending the classes, but frankly I "needed" their company and a distraction from my life at the time. And so, I went to every class.

I didn't share what I was going through! Of course not! After all, they had their own shit to contend with! I didn't want to burden them with my crap, especially during our happy time. And anyway, I *should* be able to figure it all out by myself! Right!?! I considered myself a great craftswoman. After all, I used to run my own craft shop. So then, I should ace this, right!?! **Wrong!!!...**

What I did receive was a great gift. And it didn't have anything to do with beading either. I am grateful beyond measure, that I stuck it out and continued the classes. If it had not been for the intimate setting in the home of my dear friend, and the inclusive company of my soul sisters, I likely would have not gone at all, or would certainly have quit after the first session. But I persisted.

The wind-catcher hanging I produced accurately illustrated my journey at that time. The first week, in the spell of overwhelm, I could not do it. My fingers bled. I felt (inwardly) angry and frustrated. The patient, calm and loving soul sister who was teaching us, tried in her way to help me in my efforts. Then, after tea break, she just let me do my own thing.

Interesting, those first few classes, how my efforts produced stiff, unbending strands. They would likely never bend in even a gale force wind. A striking contrast to the loose, flowing, beautiful strands the others were creating!

When the classes began I, like my strands of wire-wrapped beads was rigid and unbending. In my pain, life controlled me. I did not control life. Over the next weeks, as I meditated, prayed, and let go, a bit at a time, my strands became freer. Our beautiful instructor commented that she saw the progress I was making.

Finally, I was able to *detach* from outer circumstances, to see the gifts, to forgive, let go and allow. I felt gratitude instead of pain, anger and fear.

And lo and behold, I spent a couple of glorious days, happily and freely redoing those strands. Awesome! Great job! Now, they sway gently, moving with the breezes. I had remembered the gifts of allowing things to just "be." How freeing to just accept, forgive and know that all is as it is meant to be! To move bravely and boldly forward, it is imperative to leave the past in the past. Part of this process is forgiveness.

It is far too common in most of our lives, to hold onto anger, fear and other negative emotions, sometimes carrying a grudge toward others, or playing the blame game for years. We feel all self righteous and may even gossip about the perceived misdeeds here and there. Familiar patterns, _yes_. Wise or helpful, _no_!

Much more helpful on our own journey and theirs, to accept those past experiences for what they were (_past_), forgive (_present_), and free ourselves to move onward (_future_). Choose to act, rather than re-act from now on. Forgiveness is free. As well, it sets you free!

Seeing Clearly

sometimes scabs heal without scars

even seemingly deep wounds impart their wisdom

and spontaneously depart with no outward sign

they were ever there at all

this is true even in desperate situations

when you thought you would never be whole again

pain of betrayal bleeding into the deepest part of you

consuming you, stealing your present moments

in a sea of rage and resentment of epic proportions

after a while light and love

the true essence of all beings

enters the wounded one

allows you to at last see clearly

without judgement or regret

and focus only on the now

unencumbered by the crushing

weight of being in the right

and the pain of anger

forgiveness is found

the heart is healed

and peace returns

Women's Lib?... a Bit of Herstory

We have looked at a myriad of examples of gender-based inequalities, and disempowerment of women, over many centuries and in many cultures. Even with whatever strides have been made, in efforts to restore women to an equal place beside men, there is still much to be done.

So, what then is *"Women's Liberation"*? It is a noun which describes a movement to combat gender-based discrimination and to gain full legal, economic, vocational, educational and social rights and opportunities for women, in *short gender equality in all areas*. Ever since the days long ago, when God became a paternalistic male, and Goddess became disinherited, women have striven to regain a place of equality. This is not new. It has just been (largely) underreported and suppressed.

The *Suffragette Movement* began in the 1800's, as a way to allow women to vote, control their own finances and be recognized as fully independent citizens, with the same rights as men. At that time, no woman could speak publicly, unless accompanied by and approved of by her husband. They could however, sing in public, as many women sang in church choirs, which was considered an appropriate and worthy service. And so, many brave women sang their whole speeches for the cause. Resourceful!?! Absolutely! And legal too! They often were met with fierce opposition from men, and from more conservative women, who were entrenched in religious and social traditions, that taught them "a women's place is in the home." Period!

Over the last century or so, we have seen some hard-won changes in the status of women. It has been less than 100 years, since women were even considered "persons" in legal terms. In Canada a man could legally beat his wife with a stick no bigger around than his thumb (The Rule of Thumb) until 1928. Only in 1929 were they considered "persons" under the law. It was as late as 1964 in the province of Quebec, that married women could legally buy land or enter legal agreements, independently of their husbands. And the rights of women of color and all minority group citizens are coming about much more slowly than those of their white counterparts. Similarly, in the USA and on the world-wide stage.

In 1963, Betty Friedan's book "The Feminine Mystique" *opened the* floodgates on the Women's Liberation issue. It spawned further recognition of the limited opportunities women really had. Women's newspapers, bookstores and cafes opened. Birth control, family planning, abortion clinics, rape crisis hotlines, and battered women's shelters became available for women of all income levels. With higher education and birth control available, women tended to marry later and postpone childbearing.

On October 24, 1975, the women of Iceland went on strike for equal rights. Some ninety percent of women walked out of their jobs and their homes. This shut down the entire country! The men could barely cope when they had to pick up the slack left by the absentee women! The very next year, the parliament of Iceland enacted a law dictating equal pay for equal work. And five years later, Iceland elected its first female president.

In the paternalistic culture that has dominated our world for centuries, times are slow to change. More and more solid evidence has and is surfacing that refutes the long accepted religious doctrines, as discussed throughout this book. And (for the most part) it is currently safe to question the *"infallibility"* of religious dogma.

It is with no end of wonderment, that I find the Goddess-centred cultures of old, did not respect the women in their lives more! These were their mothers, their wives, the medicine carriers, the life givers. All over the world, the divine was seen as a great Creator-Goddess. And yet, on the human plane, men dominated, and culture by culture, replaced the Earth-centred Creator-Goddess (female), with a male God who lived somewhere far away!

Herein, I share the tales of two of my ancestral women. Each is at a different end of the power spectrum. As stated, (much) earlier in the book, the ancestral women in my family are of varied backgrounds. They include slaves, concubines, queens, cleopatras, teachers, healers, shaman and seers. They hale from diverse cultures and climates. Every one of us can "feel" a bit of them within us if we try.

Dinah:

The first of these is chronicled in the Old Testament of the Christian Bible, in the book of Genesis. It is the story of Dinah. Her father was Jacob (Judah) (1837-1689 B.C.), the son of the prophet Isaac and the twin brother of Esau. Her mother was Leah (Rachael), daughter of Laban (1848-1745 B.C.), the first wife of Jacob. Dinah had twelve older brothers, who would later become the patriarchs of the Twelve Tribes of Israel. She lived from 1783- 1683 B.C. She was a descendant of several of Noah and Miriam's grandsons, namely Elam (Shem), Canaan (Ham), Arphaxad (Shem), Nimrod/ Nebrod (Ham), Cush (Ham) and Tiras (Japheth). So, she was not only an ancestor of Yeshua, but also of his wife, Mary of Bethany (Magdalene). She was my 87th Great Aunt.

Genesis tells us the story of a young Dinah, going out to visit the women of the kingdom of Shechem in nearby Canaan. When she was there, Genesis tells us that Prince Shechem, son of King Hamor, saw Dinah and wanted her for his own. So, he kidnapped her, taking her by force, and raped her. He refused to let her go, keeping her in his home. It was discovered that she was pregnant by her captor. Being very much in love with the beautiful young Dinah, he sent word to her father in Judea, asking that he be permitted to marry her.

Genesis goes on to say that two of her brothers, Simeon, aged 14 years and Levi, aged 13 years, were furious that their sister had been violated without first asking their father for her hand. And so, they undertook the following rather elaborate plot for revenge. The two brothers, not much more than boys themselves, travelled to the kingdom of Shechem to settle the matter. The young prince still wanted Dinah's hand in marriage. So, the brothers told him the following. In order to lay with a woman of the tribes of Abraham, a man must first be circumcised. In this case, as wrong had been done, not only young Shechem must be circumcised, but also his father and all the men in the whole kingdom. *The deal was struck and incredibly, according to scripture, it was carried out.*

On the third day, when the men were very sore and vulnerable, the brothers and their supporters swept in and slew them all, including Shechem and Hamor. *"The Testament of the Patriarchs"*, a respected religious document says the revenge plot is okay because *"an angel instructed Levi to take revenge on Shechem for the rape of Dinah."*

It is said that Dinah refused to leave and return home as an unmarried woman who was with child. *The shame would have been too great for her to bear, even though the pregnancy was the result of violence and rape.* She insisted her brother Simeon marry her before she would go. And, so it was. The son she later delivered, called Saul, is counted as an offspring of Simeon, and even as his heir. Later, Genesis tells us, she was married to Job.

Rabbinical scriptures called *"Midrash"*, blame Dinah's act of going out into the city and exposing herself to the risk of rape, as the reason for what happened to her. What!?!? *Blaming the Victim* thinking is wrong on so many levels!! It excuses the rapist from responsibility for his actions. Then, when she stays with the prince, they call her *"the Canaanite Woman"* and again blame her for the predicament she finds herself in. *Did they think she had any choices given to her?* Remember, she was the victim of a violent abduction! And, she was the survivor of rape, held against her will and violated repeatedly! *Never once, does the Bible give Dinah herself a voice! Never does it allow her to speak about the violent events to which she was subjected. Or the resultant pregnancy, to the return home, to any of it!*

We are not so evolved even today. I clearly remember, not too many years ago, a rapist going free. and the judge admonishing the raped woman for going out at night and for wearing *"suggestive clothing"* that would tempt any man. Often, a woman *"asks for it"* if she has been consuming alcohol or substances while out socially. On the contrary, in a recent court case a local rapist used the fact that he was *"too drunk to remember"* drugging and raping a woman, as his defence. His lawyer told the court such behavior was *"not his usual way of conducting himself." The case dragged on and on, subjecting the survivor to repeating herself over and over about the details, and calling her character into question. She was so traumatized, she requires extensive counselling and support, which is still ongoing today. In the end, the judge handed out a lenient sentence to be served on weekends, so the rapist could go to work and be with his family on weekdays.* There is still a lot to be done to balance the scales!

Hatshepsut:

On quite the other end of the spectrum, we find *Pharaoh/ King Hatshepsut of Egypt, who lived from 1555-1482 B.C.* I well remember studying this ancient queen many years ago in school. Something about her caught my attention then, and held it for all these years. Of course, then I didn't (consciously) know she was my 88th great grandmother. I was pretty excited when she popped up on my genetic tree! Let's look at her life and times.

Hatshepsut was the daughter of Pharaoh Thutmosis I and his *Great Royal Wife*, Queen Ahmose. Her name translates as *"Foremost of Noble Ladies."* There were a few rumors floating about at the time, that she was actually the child of the god Amun-Ra himself, and that he had blessed Queen Ahmose with his seed to impregnate her. It was said, that she was therefore very special, and destined for greatness. *A bit far-fetched!?! Wait now! Not so different from similar claims of Divine Births in other cultures! Perhaps this very noteworthy woman may have also been a part of the Great Plan talked about earlier? She was after all, an ancestor of Mother Mary, Youssef, and therefore Yeshua himself! In any case, she was destined for greatness. And one thing is for sure, she did live in unprecedented fashion!*

As customary, Hatshepsut grew up and married her half-brother Thutmosis II, son of her father and his *Lesser Wife*, Mutnofret. Together, they had one daughter, Neferure, but no son. When their father died, her husband was named Pharaoh. He only ruled Egypt for a short time before he too passed away. And so, the official title of Pharaoh fell to Thutmosis III, a son born to Hatshepsut's husband and a member of his harem, named Isis.

As he was still just an infant, and much too young to rule, his duties were carried out by Hatshepsut, as Regent. Her daughter Neferure held the title of *"Queen"* for religious and/

or civil ceremonies. She also became his wife, in order to confirm his right to the throne, as his mother was not of royal blood. As the daughter of a royal household, this gave Thutmosis III's claim to the throne credibility. Egypt's royal lineage was matrilineal at that time.

Somewhere around the seventh year of her role as Regent things changed, and Hatshepsut stepped into her role as Pharaoh of Egypt. At the time of her coronation, she took the name *"Ma'atkare"* which translated as *"Truth is the Soul of Ra."* She began to appear in the traditional garb of Pharaoh/ King. She adopted the Khat head scarf, the Nemes headdress, the shenyt kilt and the false beard of Pharaoh/ King. She ruled well for some twenty-one years, until her death. This, in spite of the fact, that her young nephew was officially co-ruler along-side her. It is apparent though, that he was secondary to his aunt in power and control of Egypt, even as he grew into adulthood. She chose her officials well, and they supported her role as *"Pharaoh/ King."*

Although Egypt was well known for warring with its neighbors to finance its great empire-building and the running of its affairs, Pharaoh/ King Hatshepsut preferred trading with them instead. She was well respected as a strong leader, as evidenced by the fact that, there was no real discord between Egypt and other countries during her rule. She spent a great deal of time and resources in restoring damaged buildings and monuments, and creating more. She was a great patron to the arts and culture. She built chapels and temples to Amun, Hathor, Anubis and the royal ancestors. In Thebes, she built temples to honor her divine father, Amun-Re, Egypt's national god. In Karnak, she remodelled the memorial hall of her earthly father, Thutmosis II and added a barque shrine, the Red Chapel. Her supreme achievement was her own funerary monument, the *Dayr al Bahri Temple. Here, she was laid to rest with full honors in the Valley of the Kings, next to her father.*

After her death, her nephew Thutmosis III attempted to remove all evidence of his aunt's great accomplishments. He tried to give credit to his father and other men, for them. He even ordered her name removed from the *Registry of Pharaohs' Names.* Many of her monuments were defaced and/ or destroyed. However, Pharaoh/ King Hatshepsut's legacy remains. This remarkable woman ruled as Pharaoh/ King of Egypt for over twenty-one years. It was a time of peace and prosperity unequaled in this ancient kingdom. There were only a very few women, who ever achieved kingship in this patriarchal society.

A remarkable woman. A remarkable legacy.

The Bigger Picture:

Sometimes we knowingly/ purposely gravitate toward things/ places/ people with whom we have a history of negative experience. Well, why would we do so, knowing we will 99.999% repeat the historicity of it all!?! Habit? Stupidity? Desire for painful emotions? Because it's just what we do? Out of caring for the other person? Because of the 0.001% possibility of change? We all get to this place every so often. Is it going to be different this time?

It's right there, in front of you rearing its ugly trauma and drama, daring a response. You want to run away. And yet, this time you stop yourself. "If it's to be, it's up to me. It is I who creates my reality, one moment at a time. Choices made are the creators of my reality." And so, this is what I say to you.....

When it arises, welcome it all! Do not judge what is good (God), bad or otherwise. Take it inside to your heart-space and feel it fully. As it is. Allow it to resonate, ruminate, radiate, and finally, after all of that, allow it to rest. Be in there with it for a while. Quietly...

And then, just relax into the silent spaces. Dip down deeper and deeper inside your heart-space. All is well. You are safe in there. Ask your true self (your soul self) if there is something you need to learn before you can process all that trauma and drama. Trust the answer(s) you receive.

Heed the small voice in there. This is YOUR voice. This is GOD'S voice. It has been in there all along. And it will never steer you wrong if/ when you choose to truly plug into God/ Goddess/Allah/ Creator. *You ARE God/ Goddess/ Allah/ Creator!* Know this. It is true! It always was, is and ever shall be so. The divine is beyond race, gender, culture, clan or caste.

Yeshua said he was not interested in an earthly crown (although he was heir to one). He said; "The kingdom of heaven is at hand." He was "the Christ" ... "the Awakened One." His was an *inner kingdom.* "Heaven" is found deep within the human heart. All of us are capable and worthy of entering in, without priests, shaman and other types of gurus to lead us there. That is what he was trying to tell us! It takes time and effort on our part. And it is 100% doable. Too many people have and do make too much money to wish us to know this simple fact of (human) life.

Neal Donald Walsh, author of the "Conversations with God" series of books, says we are a very young species, in an early childhood stage of development. Excellent! Just think of the possibilities and the probabilities for growth, learning and advancement on all levels of our beingness! There is no end in sight! Only that which we ourselves place there by mis-take! No matter who, how, where you are, to requote my magical son; "It's all good!"

**"Sometimes in order to be truly happy,
you have to be willing to give up all hope for a better past."
...... William Holden**

"Do'st thy light not shine equally upon all beings child?"

How do you mean Master?

"For this I say onto you. Sometimes, it is not so much that ye have wished harm, but that ye have not wished well. By ignoring the plight of your neighbor, ye have turned your light away from him. I say this. Even a thought and a prayerful blessing are of great power. If that is what ye can do... then do that! For ye are more powerful than ye know."

How will that help Master?

"Verily, I say this unto you Little One. There are no bounds to your power, only those which you yourself are now choosing to create. It has always been that way! Do ye not at last see this? For I tell you it is true. Hear me now! So many of you struggle endlessly and feel powerless to change your circumstances.

I say unto you. The least ye do to benefit others, ye do for me. Consider the great suffering I was willing to undergo to do my work. Ye are not asked to do these things. Listen. Look. Love one another as thyself. That is all for now."

Yeshua/ Jesus son of Youssef and Mary...... in meditation

References and Related Reading

These books and audio-visual materials are on a variety of subjects and from a variety of viewpoints. They are arranged in no particular order. This is a starting point only, as many other excellent sources of equally valid materials exist! I have not reviewed all of these publications, and have merely compiled this list. I do not endorse any in particular, as more valid than others, and leave it to you, the reader to decide.

Life & Teaching of the Masters of the Far East Volume 1-5: by Baird T. Spalding; DeVorss & Co.

Moments of Grace: by Neale Donald Walsh; Hampton Roads Publishing Company, Inc.

Time of the Sixth Sun: by Nikki "Luna" Williams & Theo van Dort; Worldwide Productions

Prayers of the Cosmos: Commentary and Translation by Neil Douglas-Klotz; HarperCollins

The Hidden Gospel: by Neil Douglas-Klotz; Theosophical Publishing House

Start With Why: by Simon Sinek; Portfolio/ Penguin Publishing Group

Anna, Grandmother of Jesus: by Claire Heartsong; Hay House Publishing

Anna, the Voice of the Magdalenes: by Claire Heartsong; Hay House Publishing

Seven Fallen Feathers: by Tanya Talaga; House of Anansi Press

Stop Being Mean to Yourself: by Melody Beattie; Hazelden Publishing

The Dark Side of the Light Chasers: by Debbie Ford; Riverhead Books/ Berkley Publishing Group

Am I Being Kind: by Michael J. Chase; Hay House Publishing

40 Day Mind Fast Soul Feast: by Michael Bernard Beckwith; Agape Media International

The Spontaneous Healing of Belief: by Gregg Braden; Hay House Publishing

The Biology of Belief: by Bruce Lipton, Ph.D.; Hay House Publishing

Black Elk Speaks: by John G. Neihardt; University of Nebraska Press

Spiritual Liberation: by Michael Bernard Beckwith; Agape Media International

The Gospel of The Beloved Companion: by Jehanne De Quillan; Editions Athara

Limitless: by Jim Kwik; Hay House Publishing

Mary Magdalene Revealed: by Meggan Watterson; Hay House Publishing

Forgiveness: by Dr. Sidney B. Simon and Suzanne Simon; Warner Books

Illustrations-Art Work

1/ Cover Art: **"Sharing Light"** … by Sarah Mary Star, c.2017, in private collection

2/ **"Leap of Faith"** … by Andrea Wolfe, c. 2017, in private collection

3/ "**Landscape With Open Gate"** … by Pieter Molijnc, c.1630-1635, National Gallery of Art, Washington, D.C., public domain

4/ **"Head of the Virgin"** … by Leonardo da Vinci, c. 1510-1513, Metropolitan Museum of Art, NYC, public domain

5/ **"Head of Christ, Study for the Last Supper"** …by Leonardo da Vinci, c.1495, collection of Pinacoteca di Brera, public domain

6/ **"Portrait of Mary Magdalene"** … by Pietro Perugino, c. 1500, National Gallery of Art, Washington, D.C., public domain

7/ **"Jesus and Mary Magdalene"** … artist unknown, courtesy of Pixaby License

8/ **"The Magdalen"** … by Bernadino Luini, c.1525, National Gallery of Art, Washington, D.C., public domain

9/ **"Cleopatra VII"** stone bust, British Museum, London, fair use image, courtesy of MyMacedonia.net

10/ **"Peaceful Heart"** …by Andrea Wolfe, c.2016, in private collection

Printed in the United States
by Baker & Taylor Publisher Services